W9-CAU-636

SPORTS IMMORTALS
STORIES OF INSPIRATION AND ACHIEVEMENT

The rewards from sports dwell far deeper than the satisfaction of victory. They manifest themselves in the teaching of sportsmanship, teamwork, and self-sacrifice.

—Joel Platt
Sports Immortals Founder

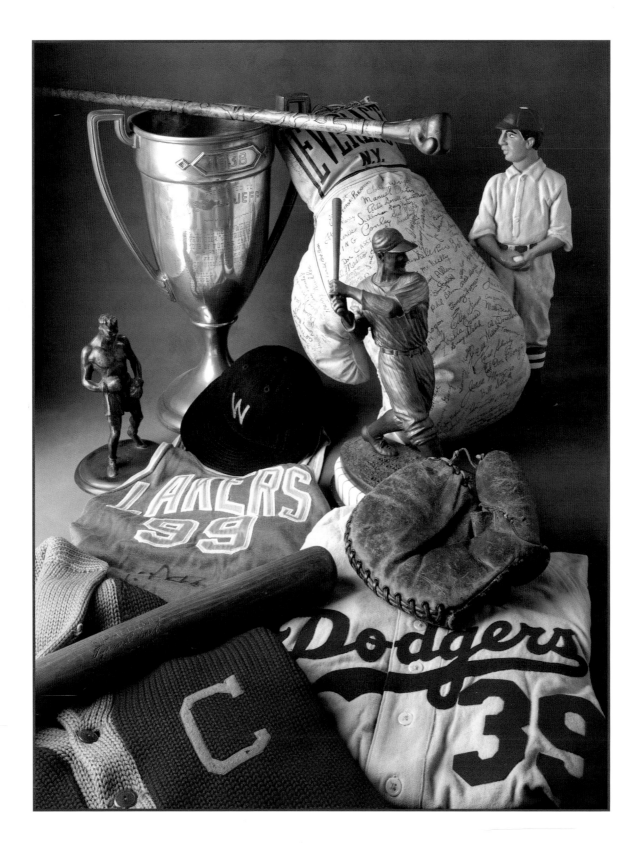

Featuring Joel Platt and the World's Largest Collection of Sports Memorabilia

SPORTS IMMORTALS
STORIES OF INSPIRATION AND ACHIEVEMENT

Jim Platt

with James Buckley Jr.

Photographs by Matt Silk

TRIUMPH
BOOKS
CHICAGO

Produced by
SHORELINE PUBLISHING GROUP LLC
Santa Barbara, California
Editorial Director: James Buckley Jr.
Designer: Eileen Wagner
Additional text: Jim Gigliotti
Memorabilia photography: Matt Silk
Other photos: Cover (Ali, Jordan, Robinson), 8, 136, 152: AP/Wide World.

Copyright © 2002 by Sports Immortals, Inc.

No part of this publication may be reproduced, stored in a retrieval system, or transmitted, in any form by any means, electronic, mechanical, photocopying, or otherwise, without the prior written permission of the publisher.

Library of Congress Cataloging-in-Publication Data

Platt, Jim, 1972–
        Sports immortals : stories of inspiration and achievement / Jim Platt with
    James Buckley Jr. ; photographs by Matt Silk.
                p. cm.
    Includes index.
    ISBN 1-57243-460-0 (hc)
        1. Athletes—Biography. 2. Sports—Collectibles. I. Buckley, James, Jr. II. Title.

    GV697.A1 P544 2002
    796'.092'2—dc21
    [B]

                                                                2002020006

This book is available in quantity at special discounts for your group or organization.
For further information, contact:

Triumph Books
601 South LaSalle Street
Suite 500
Chicago, Illinois 60605
(312) 939-3330
Fax (312) 663-3557

Printed in Hong Kong
ISBN 1-57243-460-0

Contents

Dedicated with gratitude to Edward Calesa,
whose generosity made this book a reality.
For more about Mr. Calesa's
own inspirational story, please see page 176.

————————————

To Bob Platt
You ignited Joel's passion through your incredible sports stories.
Without you, Sports Immortals would not be possible.

To Madylene Platt
Thank you for your compassion and support. Your belief in Joel's
dream helped make it come to fruition.

To Joel Platt
You are truly the greatest. Your dedication and enthusiasm
are unparalleled. I hope all your dreams come true!

To Marcia Platt
Thank you for all your love, patience, tolerance, and support.

To Dalia Platt
Thank you for your sincerity and kindness, and for inspiring me
to be the best person I can be. You truly are a treasure . . . TEMA.

To Yuri Liaboh, Robert Stephen Simon, and Ron Mahoney
Your artistic contributions are greatly appreciated.

Foreword: Franco Harris

I first met Joel Platt outside Three Rivers Stadium in Pittsburgh when I was playing with the Steelers. At first I thought he was just another fan hoping to get an autograph. However, after talking with Joel for a few minutes, I knew instantly that he was not just a collector, but a man on a mission. He invited me to his house to see the Sports Immortals collection.

After experiencing it first hand, I was blown away. Hearing about the accomplishments of great athletes was one thing, but seeing their memorabilia made it more real. In a way, for that moment, you felt as if you were part of their lives. Then, to hear Joel's personal story was even more amazing, to learn what he had overcome and how he persevered to make his dream come true. It was truly inspiring to meet someone with such a vision.

Joel was involved in collecting sports memorabilia long before people realized its historic importance. He was a pioneer and what he did could not happen today. A lot of people are collecting now, of course, and it has become a big business. But Joel's motivation was not *profit*, it was love. That's what has made all the difference.

I am impressed by Joel's enthusiasm and dedication to perpetuate the memories and achievements of the greatest athletes of all time through the future Sports Immortals Museum. I'm very proud and happy to help him in any way I can.

The Sports Immortals message has to get out. People need to experience and enjoy the collection and be motivated by what Joel has done. This wonderful book is the first step in making that happen. I think it can have tremendous influence and appeal not to only sports enthusiasts, but to all mankind. Everyone who reads it can benefit from the lessons and inspirations in these stories. Having knowledge of the past can help you make the most of your future.

When I was a kid, I went to see the Phillies once a year. I ran into the ballpark and got close to the dugout. Being near the athletes was what it was all about. Through this collection and this book, there is a way to get close to players again, especially the outstanding athletes of the past. When you see the collection and read these stories, you'll be that little kid again, running down the steps to meet your heroes.

Joel has done a wonderful thing. I am in awe of how many people he has come into contact with and how much his passion has driven him to never lose site of the ultimate dream . . . The Sports Immortals Museum. I often wonder how one man could have done so much.

I'm just very glad that he did. You will be, too.

Foreword: Maurice Lucas

If God has a better collection of sports memorabilia, He has kept it for Himself. It is with honor and joy that I write a Foreword to this amazing Sports Immortals collection.

I was introduced to Joel Platt and his world of sports memorabilia in 1970, when I was a junior in high school. At first I could not comprehend anyone curating a million sports mementos. When I finally got to see the collection, I was simply stunned.

Growing up in Pittsburgh, my baseball heroes were Roberto Clemente and Josh Gibson. Joel had a number of items from these two stars, as well as hundreds of thousands of items from other sports greats. I was completely blown off my feet and felt like the luckiest young man in town. I had the opportunity to touch items that these Sports Immortals once wore or used.

Muhammad Ali, Babe Ruth, Jackie Robinson, Wilt Chamberlain, Bill Russell, Willie Mays, Jack Johnson, Pelé, Jim Thorpe, Satchel Paige, Jack Dempsey, Joe Louis, Red Grange, and Bobby Jones . . . they were just a few of the Immortals who spoke to me with a powerful and embracing spirit that moved my heart and clarified my thoughts and inspirations to become a great athlete.

I was proud to have a chance to contribute to the collection when I received the uniform and varsity sweater of former NBA star Maurice Stokes, another Pittsburgh hero. I was tickled pink to get the uniforms, but I certainly wanted the world to enjoy them as well, so I'm pleased that they are also now part of the Sports Immortals collection.

The determination and passion that Joel has demonstrated is unsurpassed. He has dedicated his life to preserving the memories of sports legends.

Imagine for a second traveling the world and meeting some of the greatest athletes and their families and becoming the keeper of their most cherished keepsakes. The reason the families entrusted Joel with these most precious collections is so the rest of the world could see and enjoy these items. If history and/or sports are your thing, this collection is by far the greatest. It is the one you must see. The collection will be the nucleus for creating a museum that will honor the greatest athletes in sports history.

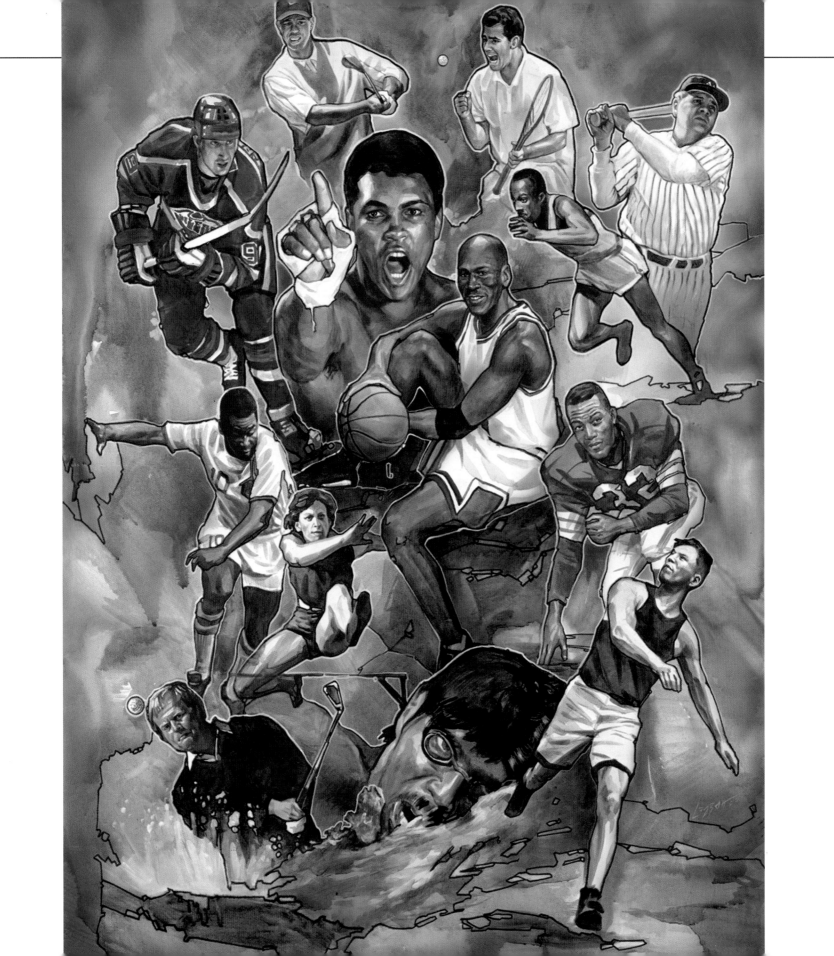

What Is Sports Immortals?

The power of sports lies in the ability of athletes to rise above the challenge of their competitors and captivate humanity. With their universal appeal, sports have the potential to transcend race, color, nationality, and borders to unite the world on a spiritual level.

For as long as anybody can remember, no one area has so perennially affected our lives as much as sports. From the chariot races in the Roman Colosseum in 80 B.C. to the unforgettable moment when Muhammad Ali ignited the torch at the Summer Olympics in 1996, sports have not only provided a vehicle for the healthy spirit of competition, but also a stage on which heroes can emerge. It is in the stadiums and arenas of history and the present that these titans of talent appear. The ballpark is their Mount Olympus . . . sports is how they display their power . . . and Sports Immortals is how they will forever be remembered.

What is it about these few individuals that make them legendary? Is it their mental and physical prowess on the field, the statistics that describe their accomplishments, or simply their unique ability to achieve peak performance in the

▲ Joel Platt grew up in Pittsburgh, and among his heroes was Hall of Fame outfielder Roberto Clemente of the Pirates (top). In his travels, Joel has met hundreds of sports legends, including Muhammad Ali (above).

◄ On the opposite page is a painting by Yuri Liaboh featuring some of the 20ᵗʰ century's greatest athletes.

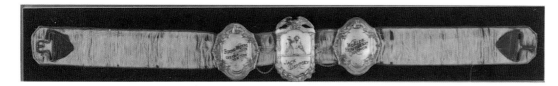

◄ Sports Immortals boasts more than 100,000 pieces of boxing memorabilia. This championship belt was awarded to the legendary Jack Dempsey.

competitive arena? No matter how athletes attain this status, one thing is certain: they are all instilled with a talent that enables them to reach a level of greatness, surpassing the accepted threshold considered to be the limit of the common person. Through the manifestation of their God-given abilities, these competitors touch the hearts of mankind and allow us to share vicariously in their victories.

The term *immortal* implies the ability to live forever. To be considered a "Sports Immortal" means that an athlete's memories and achievements will transcend the test of time and always be remembered in our minds. However, memories can fade. Unless we are reminded of these legendary heroes, it is possible that we would forget the tremendous social impact that these men and women have had on our lives. How can we keep that from happening? How can we keep the memories of special athletes and their achievements as fresh tomorrow as they are today?

One special individual had the foresight at a very young age to realize the consequences if these seemingly timeless warriors of sport were to leave our minds without a trace.

This unique individual is my father, Joel Platt, and the encouraging story you are about to read relates one man's love and dedication to the preservation of sports history. After surviving a near life-threatening explosion as a child, Joel realized his mission and set

▼ The Joe DiMaggio game bat on the left is signed by every player in the 1939 American League. The Johnny Mize model features autographs from the entire National League from that same year, in which baseball celebrated its "centennial."

▲ This 1948 program from a Joe Louis vs. Jersey Joe Walcott fight is one of thousands of original programs in the Sports Immortals collection.

out on a life-long journey, never losing sight of his dream.

As we continue into the new millennium, now is the perfect time for this book. Too often through history heroic events have been forgotten

▲ This signed Jim Brown game jersey is framed with an autographed photo and football card in a tribute to one of pro football's greatest all-time players.

and the lessons learned erased. Fortunately for us, Joel Platt was determined to make sure this did not happen in the world of sports.

The section called "The Spark that Ignited the Flame" tells the remarkable story of how my father nearly died as a child, but how out of that near-tragedy came lifelong inspiration. That inspiration led to a career of more than 50 years devoted to collecting, gathering, and curating more than one million pieces of sports memorabilia. The amazing Sports Immortals collection serves to motivate mankind, to show through the artifacts of triumph that the human spirit remains the most powerful force in the world. Seeing the uniforms, equipment, photos, autographs, programs, and more are physical evidence of the feats that encouraged us and our ancestors. The mementos collected through a lifetime of love become the keys to making sports memories immortal indeed.

A mere fraction of the mighty Sports Immortals collection is used to illustrate tales of more than 60 of history's legendary and immortal athletes. Accompanying these stories, in many cases, are Joel's personal reflections from the road that he took: "A million miles for a million mementos." Through his eyes, meet again with such figures as Muhammad Ali, Jesse Owens, Roberto Clemente, Joe Louis, Sid Luckman, Arnold Palmer, Kareem Abdul-Jabbar, and many more.

Following these stories of Sports Immortals is a special "Gallery" section, featuring even more wonderful and memorable pieces from the collection. Take a walk through more than a century of sports history by seeing the best objects and memorabilia from the Sports Immortals collection. This collection, the fruit of Joel Platt's lifelong dedication, has been called ". . . absolutely the most outstanding collection on all sports . . ." by the Smithsonian Institution.

The purpose of this book and the mission of Sports Immortals is to perpetuate the memories of the greatest athletes of all time so that we may learn from their glory and imbue in ourselves the belief that we can achieve greatness. I hope it serves as an inspiration to all that in every adversity there lies an opportunity waiting to be discovered. It is up to each individual to find it.

▲ Babe Ruth autographed thousands of baseballs in his lifetime, but this might be one of the most unique. Ruth and fellow Yankees great Lou Gehrig signed this ball and dated it October 1, 1932, the day of Ruth's famous "called shot" in Game 3 of the World Series.

▲ The great Gale Sayers and the mighty Dick Butkus signed these game-used jerseys. The Sports Immortals collection boasts thousands of uniforms from the greatest stars of every sport.

▲ A lifelong devotion to preserving the memories of legendary athletes has helped Joel Platt amass a collection that includes unique items like these (clockwise from top left): Jim Thorpe's personal Olympic scrapbook; Babe Ruth's 60-home run trophy; Michael Jordan's signed rookie jersey; boxing gloves signed by dozens of champions; Lou Gehrig autographed baseball; Babe Ruth's bat; a rare and valuable Honus Wagner card; and Thorpe's Carlisle School football jersey and helmet.

The Spark that Ignited the Flame

by Jim Platt

The Sports Immortals collection is more than just a million sports mementos . . . more than paper and cloth and wood and leather. It is the physical realization of a dream, the manifestation of a lifelong quest, a quest spurred by a life filled with a love of sports.

Sports Immortals is, simply, a testament to the drive and desire of one man: Joel Platt.

Inspired by the stories his father told him as he recovered from an accidental explosion—and by a fateful visit from the Sultan of Swat—Joel began his collecting career when he was just a kid . . . and he hasn't stopped yet. Thanks, ironically, to that near-fatal accident, Joel began a life of devotion to sports, to athletes, to their gear and memories, and to the inspiration they can bring to all who watch them.

But Joel will be the first to tell you that even dreamers need all the help they can get. And for him, that help started the moment he was born.

Here is the story of the early years of the man who created Sports Immortals. These were the first, vital steps on the road he has traveled since—a million miles for a million mementos.

▲ Joel Platt's parents, Madylene and Bob Platt.

Joel was born in 1938 in Pittsburgh, the son of Bob and Madylene Platt. Thanks to his father, sports quickly became the center of Joel's universe. Bob was a die-hard fan who seldom skipped a Pirates game and missed seeing just two local boxing matches, and those only because of the births of his two children. Bob's passion was contagious, and everyone loved to hear his well-told stories of athletic heroes and events of the past. Everyone, that is, except Joel, who, like most young boys, was more interested in playing sports than listening to his father talk about them.

That, along with everything else in Joel's life, changed in the summer of 1943. Joel was supposed to be at an overnight camp in New York, but an outbreak of mumps sent all of the children home a month early. To keep the active, mischievous Joel occupied, and

▲ The 1909 world-champion Pittsburgh Pirates are featured on this unique baseball-bat-shaped fan. The Pirates great shortstop, Honus Wagner, is on the seventh panel from the left.

because she knew he loved cars, Madylene sent him to visit her brother, Milton, who owned a nearby auto dealership. Her intentions were good, but she underestimated the danger an adventurous toddler could get into on a lot full of cars.

Joel had visited the lot numerous times, but never without his parents. Not long after Joel arrived to spend the day, his uncle suddenly had to run out to help a customer. Milton told Joel to wait inside the office.

Curious and now free of adult supervision, Joel went into the garage at the back of the property and found an old junker. He discovered a pack of matches in the glove compartment; for some reason, he loved to play with them (it had been nearly a year since he had almost burned down his nursery school).

He took the matches and started to light them. One by one, he lit every match and waited to see how long he could keep the flame alive before he had to blow it out. When he was down to the last match, Joel did something that must have made sense to him, because it would have been utterly incomprehensible to an adult. He opened the gas cap of the car, lit the match, and with a twist of fate and a flick of his wrist, he threw it into the gas tank of the junker. (Joel did not realize it then, but when he reflects today upon this event, he truly believes that this was the spark that ignited his remarkable quest, one that would take him a lifetime to achieve.)

In an instant, Joel was blown out of the garage with such violent force that the doctors were not sure if he was knocked unconscious by the strength of the explosion or the impact when he landed on the ground. Upon hearing the blast, Milton's employees found the little boy lying motionless on the ground, his shirt still on fire, and flames engulfing the car.

Dumbfounded and unable to move, none of the men reacted. Suddenly, out of nowhere, a soldier miraculously appeared. He had witnessed the incident from across the street and came to the aid of the child. After dousing the flames, he scooped him up and ran to the emergency room of Children's Hospital, three blocks away. Milton arrived at the hospital shortly after and tried to thank the mysterious soldier, but Joel's uniformed savior had vanished as swiftly as he had appeared.

The little boy was in bad shape. He was placed in intensive care, with serious burns and a strange nervous reaction to the blast that had numbed his reflexes and put him in a semicomatose state.

Bob and Madylene's sports-loving son would not open his eyes for two days.

As Bob sat beside his still-silent son's bedside a few days later, he suddenly had a wonderful idea. Madylene had mentioned that the more they could keep Joel entertained and relaxed, the faster his wounds would heal. Now he realized that his lifetime love of sports could be put to a very productive use.

Bob would tell stories.

Bob Platt's life had been infused with sports from his earliest days. As a nine-year-old newspaper boy, he won a contest and earned tickets to the

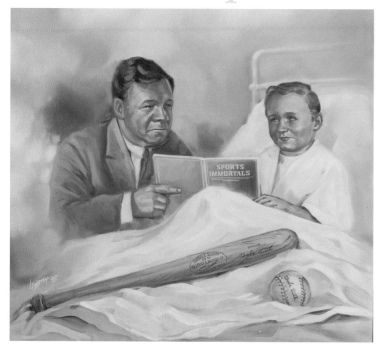

▲ Recuperating in the hospital, young Joel Platt was visited in a dream by Babe Ruth. The Bambino helped inspire Joel's lifelong desire to collect mementos from the greatest names in sports.

hold onto the ball, he placed the gift in his son's right hand and closed the fist. When he thought about how he had been inspired by watching his heroes play in 1909, he said, "Don't worry, son, someday soon you will be fielding like the Flying Dutchman and hitting like the Georgia Peach." Then he gave his son a hug. As the two embraced, their eyes connected and Bob felt the inner strength of the little boy. He was a fighter, and Bob knew that it would only be a matter of time before his condition would improve.

When Madylene arrived at the hospital early the next morning, she was pleased to find Joel awake and hanging on every word of Bob's latest story. Delighted by the scene, she kissed the two most important men in her life and let her husband finish. Soon, Bob headed for the door to leave for work. Before leaving, he turned around and put up his fists. "Tonight, Joel, we're going to talk about boxing. Later, Champ."

Madylene was thrilled; her husband had discovered a way to combat Joel's pain by telling sports stories.

▼ The Hall of Fame Pirates shortstop Honus Wagner was one of Joel's early heroes and an inspiration to the young collector's blossoming baseball career. A 1909 decal bat with Wagner's picture is shown at bottom.

1909 World Series between the Pittsburgh Pirates and the Detroit Tigers, featuring Honus Wagner and Ty Cobb. Like links in a chain, the story of Bob's trip to the World Series became the first step on Joel's road to recovery.

As Bob thought about this, Joel made a slight movement, small and whispery, but enough to make Bob jump out of the seat. He leaned over and stared into Joel's blue eyes. At first, Joel could not focus on his surroundings, but after a moment, he recognized his father and produced a fragile smile. Bob reached into his pocket and took out a brand-new baseball. Realizing that Joel could not

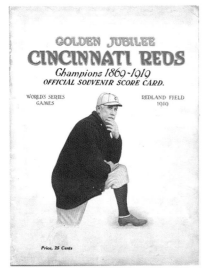

▲ From top: Ruth and Gehrig "Goudey" baseball cards; a program from the 1919 World Series; a signed photo of Pittsburgh boxing hero Harry Greb.

Meanwhile, her secret was humor and entertainment. She tried to laugh as often as possible with her little boy and constantly reminded him that he would soon be able to go home and see his friends.

That night, when Bob arrived after work, she told him, "Whatever you did last night was incredible. Please keep doing it."

"I love speaking to Joel," Bob said. "I have so much to tell him. I'm just sorry it took this injury to happen for me to be able to have the time to share my past with him."

Bob went on to tell story after story to the slowly recovering boy.

He spoke about attending the famous championship bout in 1910 between Jack Johnson and James Jeffries. Not only was it a story of great drama, but Bob wove into the tale the impact of racism on sports, and the inspiration of Johnson, a great champion who battled more than his ring opponents to succeed.

He talked about a local boxer, Harry Greb, who had been Bob's childhood pal.

"I knew him when he was a little boy growing up in Pittsburgh," Bob said. "Harry always wanted to be a boxer since he was a child. When he was eight years old, he used to put on his boxing gloves and shadow box around the living room. Then he would jump on a wooden crate, raise his hands, and yell, 'The champion of the world, Harry Greb.'"

Harry's unyielding drive and unerring pursuit of his dream (he won the light heavyweight title in 1922 by handing Gene Tunney his first and only career defeat) had an impact on young Joel, as had all the inspirational stories his father was telling him. Link by link, brick by brick, together father and son were building a dream.

Slowly, the stories, rest, and his parents' unending support helped Joel regain his reflexes. The pain lessened, and he improved continually. The end of his hospital stay was in sight, but still the stories came.

There was the tale of the 1919 World Series and a trip Bob took with his brothers to Cincinnati to see the games. To earn money for the tickets, they sold pennants, buttons, and souvenirs in the parking lot before the game. Inside the stadium, they watched in awe as the great Shoeless Joe Jackson put on a display of hitting and fielding that would eventually help mark him as one of the greatest players of all time. Bob also told the sad aftermath of the story, how a year later the White Sox became the Black Sox, when a gambling scandal linked to the Series forever branded Jackson and seven others as cheaters. But he also spoke about how he thought Jackson should be given the recognition he deserved.

Bob knew that the stories would not be enough, however, and he thought of a way to make the mental pictures he was painting for his son more real.

Not long after Joel was finally home, Bob came into the boy's room.

One of the mighty bats wielded by Babe Ruth, the great slugger who helped inspire Joel to begin his Sports Immortals collection.

"I have a surprise for you," he told his son, holding up two Goudey baseball cards. "Do you recognize these players?" Joel shook his head. He could not read their names, but was fascinated with the pictures.

Bob pointed to one and said, "This is the Sultan of Swat, and the other is the Iron Horse."

Just as Bob had hoped, Joel raised the cards close to his face and asked his father, "Pop, did you see them play?"

"I saw Babe Ruth and Lou Gehrig play in Forbes Field when the Yankees met the Pirates in the 1927 World Series. I remember seeing them take batting practice and watching the players on the Pirates stare in amazement as they saw the balls fly out of the ballpark. They ended up sweeping Pittsburgh in four games. Unfortunately, my team was no match for the Bronx Bombers."

Later, Joel's mother propped the two cards up on the bedside table so Joel could see them from where he lay in bed. One afternoon, after Joel had taken some pain medicine, he fell asleep. Moments later, as he dreamed, Joel Platt's life changed once again.

Joel heard the door open and felt the presence of a visitor. In the dark he couldn't see who it was, but he knew the man was big. The man sat in a chair next to the bed, and finally Joel saw the face.

"Babe, is that you?" he asked.

"I saw the way you looked at my card and knew I had to pay you a visit. How ya doin', Kid?" said the Babe.

"It hurts."

"Did your father talk about me?" Babe Ruth asked.

"Yes, you played on the Yankees and hit home runs."

Ruth chuckled. "That's right. I loved to hit home runs, but it didn't happen every time. Whenever I got up to the plate, I swung the bat as hard as I could. Sometimes I hit home runs. Other times I struck out, but I always gave it my best shot."

"I want to be a baseball player," Joel exclaimed.

"Kid, you can be anything you want to be if you try hard enough. Have you ever heard of Lou Gehrig?"

Pointing to his other card, Joel answered, "He was a Yankee, too, and hit home runs."

"Yes, he did hit a lot of homers, but Lou Gehrig was much more than a great hitter. He worked hard and put maximum effort into everything he did. He was a special individual both on and off the field. Everyone thought he would play

Babe Ruth hugs Lou Gehrig at the emotional ceremony held in honor of the "Iron Horse" at Yankee Stadium on July 4, 1939.

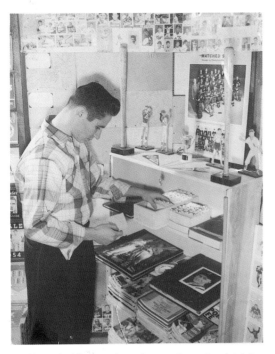

▲ Young Joel became devoted to growing and maintaining his collection from an early age.

▲ Program from September 27, 1950, fight at Yankee Stadium between Joe Louis and Ezzard Charles.

forever, but he got a rare disease [amyotrophic lateral sclerosis, known today as Lou Gehrig's disease] that eventually got the best of him.

"He fought the illness until he died in 1941, and he always had a positive attitude and never gave up. I'll never forget July 4, 1939, the day Lou said good-bye to his fans at Yankee Stadium. Lou said that although he had been given a bad break, he had an awful lot to live for.

"Do you understand what I am trying to tell you?"

Joel gave a dubious nod.

"It's easy for you to lie there and think you got a tough break with that explosion, but you've got a long life ahead of you. I see how you look at those cards and take care of them.

"Someday you might be a famous baseball player, or someday you may preserve the memories of sports legends. The future is yours, Kid. Dream big and achieve it!"

When the Babe finished his pep talk, Joel opened his eyes and leaned forward to give him a hug, but Ruth had vanished.

Joel could not believe that the encounter was a dream. It seemed so real.

It was a moment he would never forget.

Joel finally got the okay to go out and play by November, and he soon began to follow his dual dreams of becoming a major league player and honoring famous athletes. Even then, he knew that he would someday create a museum to house his ever-growing card collection. Whether it was due to the dream about Babe Ruth, or the unexplainable way the cards "spoke" to him, Joel was a boy instilled with a powerful vision.

Bob continued to fill Joel's life with sports. They went to a baseball game at Forbes Field in 1946, Joel's first view of pro players. They weren't there to see the Pirates, but rather the great Negro League team the Homestead Grays, featuring Josh Gibson and Buck Leonard.

Joel watched in amazement. Seeing a game in person confirmed his desire to be a professional baseball player. As Bob watched his son practice and work out for hours at a time, he would tell him, "Remember, Joel, you can be anything you want to be, as long as you try hard enough."

Joel stopped as soon as he heard these familiar words and tried to recall where he had heard them before. Then the dreamy image came to his mind and he smiled.

Babe Ruth.

Even though his first love was playing baseball, Joel never forgot about the dream of preserving the memories of the greatest athletes. His card collection was growing tremendously, and he soon expanded it by adding programs and books.

In 1947 Joel attended his first Pirates game, with Pittsburgh playing host to the Brooklyn Dodgers and Jackie Robinson in Jackie's barrier-breaking season. (Robinson himself was a particularly inspiring story, of course, not only to Joel as a future baseball player, but to Joel and Bob as Americans.)

Joel and Bob arrived early to Forbes Field to see batting practice. While they were watching, Bob pointed out boxer Ezzard Charles, then a top contender for the heavyweight title.

Joel looked at Charles in awe. "Gosh, he's big."

"Go ask him for an autograph," Bob said. "I'm sure he's a nice guy."

Joel was afraid at first because he had never approached an athlete in person, but he liked the idea of adding an autograph to his sports memorabilia collection. He finally walked over to the future champ, introduced himself, and asked for a signature. Charles was delighted and flattered that a young fan recognized him at a baseball game. He took the boy's pen and autographed his scorecard. Joel thanked him and returned to his seat, his huge smile showing how he felt about receiving his first autograph.

The experience taught him a valuable lesson. He realized that his request to Mr. Charles was a two-way transaction: he acquired the signature and the athlete received the recognition. By understanding this important fact, Joel's apprehension about approaching athletes went away, and he soon had another passion: collecting autographs.

He mailed dozens of stamped, self-addressed envelopes and a blank index card for athletes to sign. Shortly after, he received several autographs, including one from Joe DiMaggio.

Inspired by his success with DiMaggio, the young curator began to write to all the living Hall of Fame players requesting their signatures. His initiative paid off with signed cards from legends including Ty Cobb, Honus Wagner, George Sisler, Hugh Duffy, Cy Young, Lefty Grove, and Pie Traynor.

Meanwhile, when he wasn't working on adding to his collection, Joel continued to develop his skills on the baseball diamond. He religiously completed a daily practice schedule of running, doing push-ups and sit-ups, and throwing. In 1952, at 13, he joined a Pony League team in his neighborhood that played teams throughout the Pittsburgh area.

After overcoming a thumb injury and having to fight back into the starting lineup, Joel soon became a star on the field. The lessons he had learned about never giving up and always trying to do his best paid off with a .510 average in his first season. Some of his teammates started calling him "Young Honus," which gave him special pride.

The next year he hit .591 and was given the Most Valuable Player award. Frankie Gustine, a former All-Star third baseman for Pittsburgh and then a scout for the Pirates, thought that the young shortstop was one of the best young players he had ever

▲ Top to bottom: Joel wrote this letter to Mrs. Joe Jackson in 1951 requesting the autograph of her legendary husband; Joe Jackson's disappointing answer; signed Jackson photo that Joel received three weeks later.

▲ Young baseball star Joel Platt poses with his trophies and a photo of himself in action at Duquesne University.

seen. The following season, Joel led his team to the state championship and a spot in the Prep League World Series, to be played in nearby Munhall, Pennsylvania. Unfortunately, the hometown heroes could not advance past the quarterfinals.

In 1956 a confident Joel Platt once again led the Pittsburgh city All-Star team into the state tournament. Late in the second game of the tournament, the sun was going down on a field with no lights, and the umpires considered stopping the game. But Joel, at bat, told them to "Go ahead and pitch."

With the count 3–0, the pitcher released the ball, and Joel leaned forward to help draw the walk. Unfortunately, the pitch came in high and tight. Joel never saw the ball and it smacked him in the temple.

Unconscious, Joel lay face down on the field with blood trickling down his temple. He was out for more than five minutes, and at the hospital, was diagnosed with a brain contusion. After hours of anxious waiting, his parents were told not to worry, that Joel was going to be fine.

(Joel's bad break on the field led to a good break later on. One of the "candy striper" volunteers who worked with him at the hospital later introduced Joel to Marcia Leff, who would become his wife in 1960.)

Joel graduated high school in 1956 and went to Penn State, with the idea of playing for the Nittany Lions. But a heart attack suffered that fall by his dad, the man who was the inspiration for so much of his love for sports, gave him and his family a jolt. Joel changed plans and transferred to Duquesne University in his hometown to remain close to Bob during his recovery.

At Duquesne, Joel earned a job as the team's starting shortstop and spent the winter practicing in the gym. His dream seemed to be closer to coming true, and he worked hard to be ready to take the next step. But at the school's very first outdoor practice of the season, Joel seriously injured his throwing arm. With the snap of something in his elbow, suddenly Joel's career as a shortstop was over, though he would play the rest of the season at second base.

Following the season, doctors told Joel that he should not play again to avoid a more permanent injury. Joel was crushed. He had spent his life working toward fulfilling the dream of taking his place among the pro baseball players he so admired. And now that dream was shattered.

As the summer after that diagnosis crept by, Joel's parents became concerned that their son would not bounce back from his depression over the injury. One morning, Bob entered Joel's room and found his son staring at the Babe Ruth and Lou Gehrig cards, the original treasures of his now vast collection.

Bob reminded Joel that he had had two childhood dreams. Just because he could not fulfill one, didn't mean he shouldn't concentrate his efforts on making the second one come true. It was as if the Babe was popping back into his life with a gentle reminder. Joel knew that he still had a chance to live a dream . . . he would build a museum that would perpetuate the memories of sports greats.

For the next 40 years, nearly everything Joel did was channeled toward making that dream come true. The little boy who first traveled the pathways of the past through the words of his father became a man who would preserve that past for generations to come.

The result is the massive Sports Immortals collection, featured in this book to help illustrate the same sort of inspirational stories of great athletes and their achievements that helped young Joel first begin to live his dream.

This book shows only the tip of the iceberg of the immense collection that Joel Platt has gathered since he received those first cards from his father and those first autographs from friendly legends. The stories that accompany the items serve to demonstrate that the inspiration Joel Platt felt from hearing stories of greatness in sports can still be found in those stories today.

▲ Jim and Joel Platt with a rendering of the proposed Sports Immortals Museum. For more on the museum and the entire Sports Immortals project, please see page 174.

▲ Clockwise from top left: Arnold Palmer autographed golf ball; Stan Musial 1944 World Series jersey; Jack Dempsey's boxing gloves he wore against Georges Carpentier; Roger Maris Yankees 1961 warm-up jacket; Red Grange's leather football helmet; Wilt Chamberlain high school jersey; Muhammad Ali 1960 Olympics jersey; Bill Tilden tennis racquet; Cy Young autographed baseball; Dominik Hasek goalie stick; Dan Marino jersey; Jack Johnson 1912 fight ticket.

Sports Immortals

Baseball

▲ Clockwise from far left: Thurman Munson autographed, game-used glove; Mickey Mantle signed ball to Reggie Jackson; Nolan Ryan game jersey; Joe Jackson's "Black Betsy" decal bat; trophy given Babe Ruth for hitting 60 homers in 1927; Mel Ott game jersey; 1921 World Series pennant; signed Babe Ruth photo; Mickey Mantle "rookie" baseball card; Barry Bonds Pirates game jersey; 1933 World Series program; Mark McGwire game jersey.

Immortals Who Inspire

Here are stories of athletes whose achievement of character exceeded their achievements of skill.

Jackie Robinson

For half a century, millions of American boys who dreamed of playing in the major leagues could never realize that dream due to the color of their skin. The blatant racism of major league baseball's "color line" kept thousands of highly skilled African-American players from matching their talents against white pro players.

True, the Negro Leagues thrived for many decades as a showcase for the talents of players like Satchel Paige, Josh Gibson, Judy Johnson, Oscar Charleston, and other Hall of Famers. But many people in and out of the game were not satisfied and clamored for the color line to be broken. Two men did something more concrete about it, and one of them deservedly became a national hero.

That man was Jackie Robinson. In a move that transcended not only baseball, but all sports, and influenced the nascent civil rights movement, Robinson signed a contract to play for the Brooklyn Dodgers organization in 1945. He was signed to that contract by the team's visionary general manager, Branch Rickey, a former catcher who had already revolutionized baseball by developing the concept of the farm system. Now Rickey and Robinson would forever change the face of sports and America.

In 1946 Robinson played for the Dodgers' Montreal Royals farm club. While life in Canada was not as blatantly racist as it would be in parts of the United States, Robinson still began to face the opposition of fans and players alike. Then, in 1947, he joined the big club. His arrival in Brooklyn, where he was moved from second to first base to keep him away from the sharp spikes of opposing players, was much heralded. (He moved back to second to stay in 1948.)

And so, in the face of history, Robinson played the game. That's the simple way of saying that he put his life on the line, literally, to open the game—and in many ways, the nation—to people of all colors, races, and backgrounds. The reverberations of his courage are still felt today, an example of courage that remains among the most inspiring in sports.

Lou Gehrig

Swinging one of baseball's most-feared bats, Lou Gehrig was an inspiration for young players every time he took the field. And he gave those youngsters (and the rest of us) thrills for more consecutive games than all but one player in history.

As an example of great skill, hard work, courage, strength, and perseverance, Gehrig is unmatched.

▲ Negro League superstars including Willie Mays, Buck O'Neil, Buck Leonard, Monte Irvin, Ray Dandridge, and Leon Day signed this photo as a tribute to the great baseball and civil rights pioneer Jackie Robinson.

But while players and fans looked up to Gehrig for his ability to overcome injuries major and minor to keep alive his streak of 2,130 games, and while everyone was amazed at his feats of batting skill (see page 42-43 for more details), Gehrig was, ironically, more of an inspiration after he left the field.

In 1938 Gehrig noticed that he was slowing down, that easy grounders became trials, and that a long hit was a single rather than a double. At the beginning of the 1939 season the slowness worsened, and he finally, after more than 13 years of steady play, pulled himself out of the lineup. A visit to the Mayo Clinic soon confirmed his worst fears: Lou Gehrig was dying. He had been stricken with amyotrophic lateral sclerosis, a degenerative disease of the nerves and muscles.

The physical strength that Gehrig had used on the diamond was now turned to mental strength as he faced his fate. The reputation he had earned through hard work was burnished further by his courageous response to the diagnosis. What he called "a bad break" was a death sentence, and while most people would call him tragic, he called himself "the luckiest man on the face of the earth."

Courage comes in many forms. In sports, courage is Lou Gehrig.

▲ Lou Gehrig autographed this unique photo, taken in a lighthearted moment before a game.

Mordecai "Three Finger" Brown

A baseball player's most important physical assets are his hands and fingers. No part of the game can be successfully accomplished without dextrous skill. So when young Mordecai Brown lost the index finger of his right hand in a farming accident in which two other fingers were severely deformed, one could easily have assumed that his dream of pro baseball was lost as well.

But Brown just figured out another way to throw with his mangled hand, and boy, could he throw. The man who would become known as "Three Finger" Brown became one of baseball's greatest pitchers in the first part of the 20th century.

He overcame his injury and developed a pitching style that for many years made his curveball nearly unhittable. He turned a liability into an asset, perhaps paving the way for Jim Abbott, who succeeded in the majors in the 1990s with only one hand. Brown's lifetime ERA of 2.06 is the third-best ever, and his 1.04 ERA in 1906 was the second-best in the 1900s. He also helped the Chicago Cubs win two World Series titles.

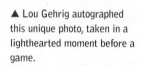

▲ Here is a rare signed baseball from the legendary "Three Finger" Brown.

Connie Mack

▲ In 1944 a host of baseball greats turned out to honor Mack on his golden anniversary in baseball. Among them were (left to right) Frankie Frisch, George Sisler, Eddie Collins, Mack, Honus Wagner, Walter Johnson, and Roger Bresnahan.

On April 26, 1901, the Philadelphia Athletics of the brand-new American League played their first game, a 5–1 loss to the Washington Senators. For the next 50 years, a lot of things would change for the A's and the A.L., but one thing remained firm and fixed: Cornelius McGillicuddy—Connie Mack to one and all—was then and would be the man in charge in Philly.

When A.L. president Ban Johnson declared that his league would henceforth be on equal footing with the established National League, Mack was hired by Ben Shibe to manage the new Philadelphia A.L. franchise. Mack, formerly among pro baseball's best-fielding catchers, was also made one of the team's owners with a share of 25 percent. But while he owned only a quarter of the team, he was 100 percent of the brains behind its play on the field.

In 1902 the club won the pennant and repeated the feat in 1905. The A's added World Series titles under Mack—who managed his games wearing not a uniform but a neat and tidy business suit—in 1910, 1911, and 1913.

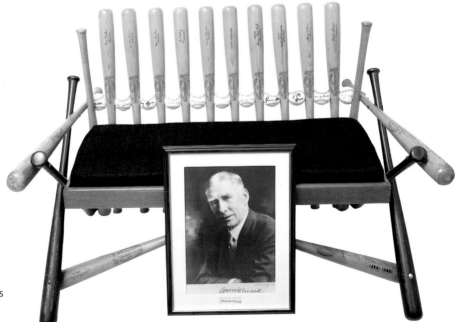

▶ This unique loveseat was presented to Mack in 1941. It was created with bats and baseballs signed by many of his greatest players.

A fallow period followed until Mack, with the help of Hall of Fame stars including Lefty Grove, Jimmie Foxx, Al Simmons, and Mickey Cochrane, resurrected the club in the late 1920s, winning three consecutive pennants and two World Series (1929–1930). Though he was inducted into the Hall of Fame in 1937 while still an active manager, Mack's clubs never again reached the top of the charts.

When he finally retired after the 1950 season, Mack had won more games than any other manager, a record he still holds today. The "Tall Tactician" also was the last of a rare breed of owner/managers. A baseball team owner would never again step into the dugout (save for a bizarre one-game stint by Atlanta's Ted Turner in 1977).

Mack's longevity, his creativity, his resourcefulness, and his unmatched ability to win in different eras mark him as a unique figure in baseball history.

▲ This is the actual document creating the Philadelphia Athletics. Among the signatures on the "Articles of Association" was that of Cornelius A. McGillicuddy.

Immortal Encounter

After searching for Connie Mack mementos for several years, I finally tracked down one of his grandsons, Tom McGillicuddy, near Atlantic City, New Jersey. I didn't get to Tom's home until 10:00 at night, but after I introduced myself and explained the reason for my visit, Tom politely invited me in.

We discussed the Sports Immortals Museum and how I was desperately looking for an item to adequately represent Connie Mack in the collection. Convinced of my sincerity and excited about the project, Tom proudly showed me the unique treasures that he had from his grandfather.

I could not believe what I saw. There were hundreds of old baseball guides dating to the 19th century, several hundred autographed bats and balls, a 1941 love seat made completely from autographed bats and balls from Connie's favorite players, the original framed articles of association for the Philadelphia Athletics, and personal scrapbooks containing signed letters to Mack from baseball greats including Ty Cobb, Babe Ruth, and Rogers Hornsby. Tom gave me a few small items that night, and we promised to keep in touch.

Over the years we became good friends, and even started a real estate company together in south Florida named C. Mack Realty. Tom holds a position on the Sports Immortals Honorary Board.

In the early 1990s, I purchased Tom's entire collection of Connie Mack memorabilia. I promised to share the items with the public so that the world would remember Connie Mack's accomplishments.   —JOEL PLATT

Cy Young

▲ There's no telling how many of Cy Young's incredible total of 511 wins these spikes were a part of, but the great pitcher actually did wear them during his career.

The New York Highlanders (later the Yankees) should have seen it coming. On June 30, 1908, the winningest pitcher in baseball history—then and now—threw the third no-hitter of his amazing career against New York. Midway through his 19th major league season, 41-year-old Denton True "Cy" Young blanked New York in an 8–0 Red Sox victory. It was the crowning achievement in one of baseball's greatest pitching careers.

Young's numbers and feats would fill volumes. Among them are an all-time record 511 victories (as well as an all-time record 316 losses); all-time records for games started (815) and innings pitched (7,356); 15 seasons with 20 or more wins; seven times leading the A.L. in shutouts; and three no-hitters, including a perfect game in 1904, the first ever pitched after new rules allowed pitchers to throw over-hand beginning in 1894.

In 1890 a tall, hard-throwing Ohio farmboy joined the Cleveland Spiders of the National League and posted a 9–7 record. He would not have a losing record for a season until 1905, and even then he was 18–19. The kid they called "Cy" (after his cyclone-speed pitches or else because of his rural upbringing) had three 30-win seasons with Cleveland and threw his first no-hitter in 1897. After two seasons with the Cardinals, in 1901 he joined the Boston franchise in the new American League (a team known as the Pilgrims, the Americans, and, beginning in 1907, the Red Sox), for whom he would lead the league in wins from 1901–1903.

Though he remained among the league's best as his career wound down, Young, at 41, was past his prime when he took the hill against New York

▼ Cy Young, baseball's all-time winningest pitcher, signed this ball.

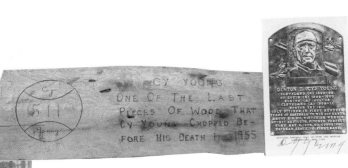

▲ Young was famously active even in his later years. The former Ohio farmhand was chopping some firewood (left) just before he died; this is one of the last pieces he chopped. His autograph is at the bottom of the postcard depicting his plaque in the Baseball Hall of Fame.

▲ Young used this cane to help him get around after his retirement. He actually once said that he was bunted into retiring. His arm was sound, but his legs wouldn't let him get off the mound quickly enough to field bunts.

that day in 1908. Prime or no prime, the old man tore the Highlanders apart and a single base on balls kept him from being the first and only pitcher with two perfect games. Young wrapped up his career in 1911 after three seasons with the Cleveland Indians.

As an exemplar of consistent excellence and endurance over time, Cy Young remains a one-of-a-kind role model for pitchers.

Cy Young, whose autograph is visible just above the word *Pilsener*, is one of a veritable galaxy of stars who signed this program from the centennial celebration of baseball in 1939. Hall of Fame signatures include Ty Cobb, Babe Ruth, Walter Johnson, Connie Mack, George Sisler, Tris Speaker, Honus Wagner, Grover Cleveland Alexander, Eddie Collins, Commissioner Ford Frick, Clark Griffith, Napoleon Lajoie, Commissioner Kenesaw Mountain Landis, and umpire Bill Klem.   ▶

Christy Mathewson

▲ Mathewson autographed this photo to his old fraternity at Bucknell University shortly before his death in 1925.

The World Series turns 100 in 2003, and in that century there have been many incredible, inspirational performances by pitchers over the years. But baseball is still waiting for a pitcher to match the feats of Christy Mathewson in the second Series ever played in 1905.

The New York Giants ace, who would become one of the first five players elected to the Hall of Fame in 1936, put on a display in 1905 that boggles the imagination. In Game 1 on October 9, he allowed only four hits and New York defeated the Philadelphia Athletics 3–0. In Game 3, played on October 12, "Matty" again gave up only four hits in a 9–0 win. Finally, in Game 5, played only two days later, the right-hander gave up only six hits, surrendered no walks, and retired the final 10 batters in order as the Giants won the game, 2–0, and the World Series. In six days Mathewson had pitched three complete-game shutouts, allowed only 14 hits, walked only one batter,

Immortal Encounter

While driving the Pennsylvania Turnpike with my wife in 1961, I took a detour to Lewisburg, Pennsylvania, to the colossal estate of Christy Mathewson's widow. I was met there by Mrs. Mathewson's sister, who was very kind, but informed me that Mrs. Mathewson could not be disturbed as she was enjoying her afternoon tea. She took my brochure and asked me to return in an hour.

When I returned, Mrs. Mathewson was waiting outside on the porch with the brochure in her hand. My wife Marcia watched from the car as I timidly climbed the steps toward the entrance. As I approached, she held her arms out to hug me.

"Oh, Joel, I've read all of this," she said. "It reminds me of my Christy. He, too, was injured in an explosion, during World War I."

She walked down to the car and insisted that Marcia come in for a visit, too. She treated us like long-lost family members.

When I said I was hoping to obtain a memento from Christy for the museum, Mrs. Mathewson led us upstairs to an old trunk that had belonged to her husband. Before turning the key, she said that it had not been opened since her husband's death 36 years earlier. I had goose bumps. My eyes opened wide and my heart began to race. She handed me a baseball autographed by Christy, the last glove that he wore, and a beautiful autographed photo. I was amazed that she was giving me all of these items. To say that I felt honored and touched was a big understatement.

Lastly, she handed me Christy's Chemical Warfare Medal (right) given for bravery in combat. The medal was extremely special, but it could not compare to Mrs. Mathewson's special words.

"My Christy was buried in his army uniform," she said. "I took this off the lapel just before they closed the casket. It is my most prized possession, and I want you to have it."

—JOEL PLATT

and struck out eighteen. While other pitchers since have won three games in a Series, Mathewson's overall record in 1905 has yet to be matched.

But that was not much of a surprise to anyone who saw him pitch. He began his big-league career in 1900, one of only a handful of former collegians to join the still somewhat second-class major leagues. He won 20 or more games 13 times and captured five N.L. ERA and strikeout titles. Mathewson relied on several different pitches, but his most famous was the "fadeaway," a type of virtually unhittable screwball.

"Mathewson was the greatest pitcher who ever lived," said Philadelphia's longtime manager Connie Mack. "It was wonderful to watch him pitch—when he wasn't pitching against you."

After his career ended in 1916, Mathewson was briefly a manager before joining the army during World War I. Sadly, he never fully recovered from a poison gas incident in the conflict and he died in 1925 at the age of 45.

But although Mathewson died early, his exploits live on, and every World Series pitcher since has been aiming at Matty's amazing 1905 success.

▲ Above: A baseball glove that Mathewson wore while playing for the Giants. Left: A ball autographed by Mathewson; note the red and blue stitching of the early 1900s ball. Below: The note from Mathewson's widow that accompanied her donation of his chemical warfare medal (opposite) to the Sports Immortals Museum.

MRS. CHRISTY MATHEWSON Sept. 1th 1961

To Joel:-
This is a pin taken from my husband (Christy Mathewson's uniform It means "Chemical Warfare Service"
Very truly
Mrs. Christy Mathewson

Honus Wagner & Ty Cobb

▲ This rare "T206" Honus Wagner card was issued by the American Tobacco Company in 1910. It is the most valuable card in the world. The card's rarity stems from Wagner's insistence that his cards be removed from the set. He didn't wish to be seen as promoting tobacco use.

As baseball enters the 21st century, the game is awash in talented shortstops, players who combine graceful fielding with powerful batting strokes. But as good as Derek Jeter, Alex Rodriguez, and Nomar Garciaparra are, tell them to check back after they've kept doing what they're doing for another 15 years. Then we'll see if they still compare to Honus Wagner.

The Pennsylvania native was one of the finest fielders ever, with remarkable range and a powerful arm; stories persist that his big hands were so anxious to get the ball to first base that he routinely sent fistfuls of dirt along with the ball.

He led the National League in hitting eight times, a feat matched only by Tony Gwynn; he also led seven times in doubles, six times in slugging percentage, and five times each in RBI and stolen bases. That latter category shows that he had another powerful weapon in his arsenal: speed. He is 10th all-time with 722 steals, and three times stole second, third, and home in one inning.

Fans of great players got a special treat in 1909, when Wagner's Pirates took on the Detroit Tigers led by Ty Cobb. (Legend says that during that Series, Cobb warned the Dutchman that he was coming down to steal second, spikes flying, and that Wagner laid him out with a hard tag. But fact disproves legend; Cobb attempted to steal second only once in the Series, which he did successfully, and Wagner

▲ Wagner used this glove in his final two seasons with Pittsburgh. He also wore the jersey at the top as a player and the other while a longtime coach for the team.

Baseball

▲ Ty Cobb posed in his Tigers uniform and a suit for these unique and rare photos. His autograph appears vertically between the two photos.

never made a tag. Cobb later wrote, however, "Spike Honus Wagner? It would have taken quite a foolhardy man.")

Led by Wagner's .333 batting average and six stolen bases and by rookie pitcher Babe Adams's three victories, the Pirates won their first world championship in seven games. It was the only time Cobb and Wagner, who would both be part of the Baseball Hall of Fame's first class in 1936, would meet on the diamond.

Wagner retired in 1917 and was later a longtime coach for the Pirates. He died in 1955, then as now the greatest shortstop ever to play the game and a true sports immortal.

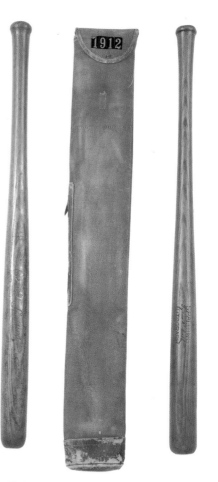

▲ Ty Cobb carried his bats, a pair of which are above, in this specially made cloth-and-leather case. He used these bats to win the 1912 batting title with a .410 average.

Immortal Encounter

On Mother's Day 1956 I decided to take my first curating trip to meet Mrs. Honus Wagner. Growing up in Pittsburgh and playing shortstop for Duquesne University, it was only natural that Honus Wagner would be my idol. My father often told me stories about Wagner's great fielding, tremendous grit, and unmatched hitting skills. He said, "Honus could scoop up anything with his huge hands.

It was midafternoon when I rang the doorbell of Mrs. Wagner's home in Carnegie, Pennsylvania. Mrs. Wagner answered the door and invited me into her home. I wished Mrs. Wagner a happy Mother's Day and presented to her a wooden ashtray depicting Honus Wagner's image with his baseball records engraved in the base. "I've never seen anything like this," she said. "It's a wonderful piece of work and I can't thank you enough for such a thoughtful gift." I mentioned to Mrs. Wagner the

admiration I had for her husband and how he was an inspiration for me as a player. We spoke for several hours about my plans to establish a museum that would honor sports immortals. "What a great idea!" Mrs. Wagner said. She left the room and returned with a bronze mold of one of Honus Wagner's tremendous hands (right).

"Please take this memento for display in your planned museum. I know Honus would have wanted you to have it." I thanked Mrs. Wagner and told her I would proudly display her gift in the Sports Immortals Museum collection. —JOEL PLATT

Walter Johnson

An Idaho telephone company's loss was baseball's gain. After being cut by a shortsighted minor league team, Walter Johnson was digging postholes for telephone poles when he was discovered by the Washington Senators, and in 1907, the legendary ride of the "Big Train" began.

Johnson employed an almost lazy-looking sidearm motion to devastating effect. Hitters knew that his famous fastball was coming, but they rarely could do anything about it. He earned his famous nickname from the sound the pitches made, which reminded batters of an oncoming locomotive.

For much of Johnson's 20-year career, all of which was spent with the usually hapless Senators, he was among baseball's dominant pitchers. He won 20 or more games 12 times, pitched a record 110 shutouts, led the A.L. in strikeouts in a remarkable dozen seasons, and won five ERA titles. His 1920 no-hitter missed being a perfect game only because of a single error. Johnson ended his long career with 417 victories—second-most of all-time—and a then-all-time-record 3,509 strikeouts.

How much of a strikeout pitcher was Johnson? On two occasions, he faced bases-loaded, no-outs situations. He got out of both by striking out the next three hitters . . . each time on nine pitches. In another game, Ray Chapman reportedly took two strikes against Johnson and then headed back toward the dugout, so sure of what would happen if he stayed.

That's power.

Because the Senators could rarely manage to win when Johnson wasn't pitching, he didn't make the World Series until 1924. Though he failed in his two starts, his four scoreless innings of relief in Game 7 helped Washington win their first pennant over the New York Giants.

▲ Johnson wore this cap during the 1925 World Series, which the Senators lost to the Pirates.

▲ This unique pin features portraits of all the members of the Pirates who defeated Johnson and the Senators in the 1925 World Series.

▲ Autographed photo of the "Big Train."

▲ A rare press pin from the 1925 Series.

Baseball

▲ A Walter Johnson game-used glove and autographed baseball.

The team returned to the Fall Classic the next year, this time facing the Pittsburgh Pirates. This time, Johnson was more successful as a starter, winning Games 1 and 4, but the team was not a winner. Leading 7–6 in the eighth inning, the Senators and Johnson gave up three runs in the bottom of the inning, unearned because of Roger Peckinpaugh's throwing error, and the Pirates came back to win 9–7.

Johnson, by then baseball's all-time strikeout king, retired two years later second only to Cy Young in career victories and still today ranked among the greatest fireballers ever to take the mound.

Let someone else dig the postholes.

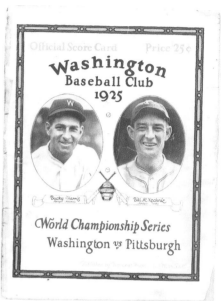

▲ An official Senators scorecard from the 1925 World Series.

Immortal Encounter

I visited Walter Johnson's family in Germantown, Maryland, hoping to obtain some mementos of the "Big Train." They all were very receptive to the Sports Immortals concept, but few had any items of tremendous value.

Finally, I met a grandson and cousin of Johnson who had some incredible pieces. They contributed the cap that Johnson wore in the 1925 World Series, along with a game-used glove and an autographed baseball.

I also had another link to the Hall of Fame pitcher: Eddie Ainsmith, Johnson's personal catcher. I went to see Eddie in Pompano Beach during the late 1970s to ask him some questions about the great hurler. As I shook his hand, I knew instantly this was a man who caught many fastballs in his day. The fingers of his huge hands were broken and swollen.

We sat and chatted for several hours about baseball before 1930. Eddie told me how spectacular Walter Johnson was as a pitcher and as a person.

"Johnson threw so hard the hitters were afraid to get up to bat," Eddie said. "When the sun began to set in the sky and the pitching mound was in the shadows, the batters' legs would tremble as they got in the box. But Johnson was such a nice guy that he would often ease up on the speed of his fastball just to let the players hit the ball."

When Eddie was finished telling baseball stories, I thanked him for his time and for all the rich information he provided. In this instance, the stories were as good as any memento I could have received for the collection.

—JOEL PLATT

Babe Ruth

Trying to describe the impact of Babe Ruth on baseball is like trying to measure the impact of Columbus on America. Baseball was around before Ruth and would be around after it, but the sport, like our continent after the age of exploration, would never be the same again. Ruth's influence on the game was enormous, lasting, and vital.

The Babe started his career as a left-handed pitcher with the Red Sox in 1915. He showed the first flashes of the slugging power that would someday help him create his own adjective, "Ruthian," by hitting 29 home runs in 1919. It was the first time he set the major league record for homers, but it wouldn't be the last.

Traded to the Yankees before the 1920 season in a sale still mourned throughout New England, Ruth led the charge as baseball took a quantum leap out of the "dead-ball era." Ruth sent 54 of the new, livelier balls out of ballparks, shattering his own record and

▲ Ruth and Lou Gehrig formed the greatest one-two punch in baseball history. The duo autographed this photo.

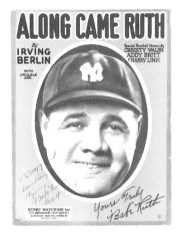

▲ As much a hero off the field as he was on it, Ruth inspired books, movies, stage shows, and even this song by famed composer Irving Berlin. The copy of the songsheet above was personally autographed by Ruth at the lower left.

Immortal Encounter

On a muggy afternoon during the summer of 1958, I arrived at the apartment where Babe Ruth's widow lived. When I knocked at the door, a maid asked me what I wanted, and I said that I had a gift for Mrs. Claire Ruth. At that moment, Mrs. Ruth came to see who was there. I introduced myself, and she invited me inside.

I took a seat in the living room and presented her with a Babe Ruth ashtray. She could not believe her eyes when I said that I had made it myself.

I told Mrs. Ruth about the brief time after my injury that I began to doubt if I would ever get better. My pain was severe, and I was taking strong medicine to suppress my discomfort. Then one day, I had a dream that Babe Ruth came to see me. It seemed so real. Babe knew of my hopes of becoming a major leaguer, but he also planted the seed in my mind that one day I should open a museum to honor sports immortals, so that the public would never forget their great accomplishments. Just before he left, he told me that I could do anything I wanted in life

as long as I put forth maximum effort and never gave up.

Mrs. Ruth was speechless. She hung on every word I was saying and told me that with my determination I could do anything I wanted to in life.

I smiled at her kind words and began to tell her the main reason for my visit. Before I could finish my sentence, Mrs. Ruth excused herself and went into the storage room. When she returned, she carried a uniform that Babe wore during his last season with the Boston Braves. She also had an autographed bat that he received as a gift. "Babe used to practice his swing with it," she said. "It was one of his favorite treasures." Lastly, she held a plaque that Babe was given in 1947, the year before he died.

I did not know how to thank her. She sensed I was having trouble finding the right words and said: "Like my Babe would have said, 'Kid, when all of Babe's things are on display in your museum, that will be my real thanks.'"

—JOEL PLATT

▲ Frankie Frisch, Gabby Hartnett, and Billy Herman are a few of the former stars whose signatures join Ruth's on this jersey the Babe wore during an Old-Timers' Game held after Ruth left the playing field behind. Also shown is an autographed Babe Ruth baseball.

besting all but one other A.L. team. His .847 slugging average that year remained a record for the rest of the century, topped finally in 2001 by Barry Bonds' .863. In 1921, Ruth did even better, with 59 homers, 171 RBI, and 177 runs, perhaps the greatest single-season offensive performance ever.

In 1927 he smacked 60 home runs, instantly making that the ultimate goal for sluggers and a record that would stand until 1961. He finished his career in 1935 with 714 home runs. At the time, no other player had 500, and his record would last until 1974, when it was broken by Hank Aaron.

But while Ruth's feats on the field were almost beyond belief, it was his personality that had perhaps a greater impact. His larger-than-life appetites for all parts of life, good and bad, kept him in the headlines and the public eye as much as his baseball skills and feats. Ruth was perhaps America's first transcendent sports superstar, an athlete so celebrated and talked-about that he left the sports pages behind and entered the wider American consciousness.

His numbers were astounding, still used as the basic benchmarks for individual success as a hitter. Ruth is still regarded—because of his great early success on the mound combined with his hitting feats—as perhaps the greatest all-around player ever. Ruth's effect on the game, especially coming as it did in the wake of the 1919 "Black Sox" scandal, was also life-giving. Baseball moved permanently into the national picture, thanks to Ruth, as the sins of the past were forgotten and fans joyously cheered for the big man they called Babe.

▲ This bat was used by Ruth during his record-setting 1927 season. It is signed by Ruth, Lou Gehrig, and other Yankees teammates.

▼ This trophy was presented to the Babe in 1927 after he became the first player in history to hit 60 home runs in a season.

Lou Gehrig

▲ This modern bronze sculpture captures the mighty left-handed swing that helped Gehrig hit 493 homers in his career with the Yankees.

As an example of great hitting skill, as a role model for the athlete as "good guy," as an exemplar of longevity for his remarkable consecutive-games streak . . . any one of these alone would have made Lou Gehrig a legend. And indeed he was all of those things.

But it was his courage in the face of death that truly separates the "Iron Horse" from other talented and inspirational athletes.

In some athletes, we find courage for their deeds on the field, for their determination in fighting against great odds. We watch other athletes overcome pain to succeed. And in the rare case of Lou Gehrig, we see that courage and determination extend beyond the white lines and into life itself.

A slugger surpassed only by his teammate Babe Ruth, Gehrig's numbers are nearly overshadowed by his tragic story. Here's a quick reminder: .340 lifetime batting average; 1,995 RBI, third all-time; four seasons with 400-plus total bases, twice as many as any other player; A.L. single-season record 184 RBI; 47 home runs in 1927—the most ever in a season to that point, except for

◀ This collection of 1927 World Series souvenirs includes a program signed by both teams (Gehrig's signature is right below the picture of Commissioner Landis, center) and a signed photo of Yankees manager Miller Huggins. Gehrig hit .308 as the Yankees swept the Pirates.

Baseball

totals put up by Ruth; four home runs in a game in 1932; the 1934 Triple Crown; and on and on.

But beyond the numbers, fans saw a legend of longevity every time they saw the Yankees play. That's because every time the team took the field from May 31, 1925, until early 1939, Gehrig played. Through injury, pain, sickness, whatever, he played the game, a consecutive streak of 2,130 games that was not broken until 1995 by Cal Ripken Jr.

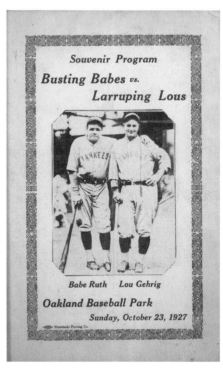

◄ Gehrig's first baseman's mitt shows just how far baseball gloves have evolved since he played. He used this mitt during the Yankees' World Series championship season of 1927.

The thing that finally drove Gehrig out of the lineup in 1939 was the same thing that took his life in 1941: amyotrophic lateral sclerosis, ALS, today known as "Lou Gehrig's Disease." Anyone who has ALS, or any terminal disease, can look to Gehrig for courage in the face of death.

"Fans, you have been reading about the bad break I got," Gehrig said at his farewell event on July 4, 1939, at Yankee Stadium, one of the most famous events in baseball history. "Yet today, I consider myself the luckiest man on the face of the Earth."

No, Lou, we—and baseball—were the lucky ones.

▲ Dozens of Hall of Famers signed this program from a dinner honoring Gehrig in 1939.

▲ Lou Gehrig used this bat to hit a double in the 1932 World Series.

▲ The offseason meant time for barnstorming. Ruth and Gehrig led teams in exhibitions nationwide.

Josh Gibson

▲ Gibson wore this Homestead Grays warm-up jacket during his career with the team from 1930–31. He also starred for the Pittsburgh Crawfords.

Writing about Josh Gibson is like writing about Paul Bunyan. The legends of each grow in the retelling, and their feats continue to defy belief. But while Bunyan was the stuff of fiction, Gibson was as real as the green outfield grass. What makes telling Gibson's story harder is that so many baseball stories rely on numbers to tell the tale. In his case, however, as with many other Negro League stars, the stats are often sketchy and unreliable. And so in steps myth.

Did Gibson really hit more than 800 home runs in his career, dwarfing Ruth and Aaron? Did he really hit a fair ball completely out of Yankee Stadium? Did he have 84 home runs in a season? (There is some dispute on that last point, but he did hit 75 in 1931, according to *Total Baseball*.)

"I broke in [to the Negro Leagues] in 1937," said Hall of Fame catcher Roy Campanella, "and there were already legends about him. Once you saw him play, you knew they were true."

Gibson combined rare power with a great batting eye, helping him win numerous league titles in both home runs and average, matching the success of a certain Yankee outfielder so closely that Gibson was often called the "Black Babe Ruth." But the player whom Satchel Paige called "the greatest hitter who ever lived" toiled his entire career away from the bright lights of the major leagues, thanks to the horrid "color line." However, in exhibition games against white players, Gibson's performances often dominated the game. Major

▼ The powerful Gibson used this Hank Greenberg-model bat to hit four home runs in a game at Yankee Stadium. The bat was autographed by Gibson and his teammates.

league players knew that Gibson had big-league talent.

"Any big-league club would love to get Gibson for $200,000," said Hall of Fame pitcher Walter Johnson, in the days when that was a lot of money for any player.

Gibson's story, already a mix of triumph and sadness, has a tragic end. In early 1947 he died at the young age of 35, still one of the best players in his league. Nearly forgotten for many years, his reputation was revived with his Hall of Fame selection in 1972, and he has since taken his rightful and deserved place among the pantheon of the greatest players of all time . . . no matter what color.

▲ One of Gibson's game-used jerseys. The Grays were based in Homestead, Pennsylvania, southeast of Pittsburgh.

Immortal Encounter

While visiting with Satchel Paige, I mentioned that I was trying to locate some mementos of Josh Gibson. Paige suggested I contact Pocahontas Crews, or "Pokey," as she was called by her friends.

Pokey was the longtime traveling secretary of the Homestead Grays and a storehouse of information about Negro League baseball and about Gibson in particular. "He was the greatest player of them all," she said. "I remember the day he hit four home runs at Yankee Stadium. One of them traveled more than 500 feet and landed in a spot nobody had ever reached before."

Pokey and I became good friends. After spending much time together, she told me about Gibson's downfall, a story to which few people had been privy.

"Josh was my favorite player," Pokey said. "He was a gentle giant who kept in great shape and never drank alcohol. Then one day, his life fell apart. We were on the road and Josh got a telegram. It was short. It said, 'Your house in Pittsburgh caught on fire—burned to the ground.' He went into shock after he read it. We all thought he was upset over the house, but it was worse. You see, Josh did not trust banks. All the money he ever made was stored in the house. His life savings went up in smoke with the rest of his things.

"After that, his nerves broke down and he began to drink. I began to get calls in the middle of the night to come get him because he was too drunk to move. I tried everything to get him to stop, but nothing worked. As time went on, his situation became worse, and his drinking continued. Finally, he died of cirrhosis of the liver. Poor Josh, my favorite man drank himself to death."

When she finished telling the story, Pokey excused herself and went into another room, where I thought she was getting a tissue. But when she returned, she was holding a huge baseball bat.

"Joel, do you remember the game I told you Josh hit four home runs at Yankee Stadium?" she said. "Well, this is the bat he used that day. It is auto-graphed by Josh and all his teammates. It is very special to me, but I want you to have it for the Sports Immortals Museum. If ever there was an athlete who deserved to be included, Josh Gibson is the man."

—JOEL PLATT

Jackie Robinson

On rare occasions, sports leaves its cloistered world and enters the wider consciousness of civilization. The games are suddenly more than just entertainment, and the men playing them become more than just athletes—they become heroes.

One such occasion, perhaps the most important in American sports history, came on April 15, 1947, when a former army lieutenant named Jack Roosevelt Robinson played a game for the Brooklyn Dodgers. Robinson was the first African American to play in the major leagues in the 20th century, breaking a color barrier that had shamed the game for a half century.

Jackie Robinson's attitude in the face of prejudice, the venom of fans and opposing players, and the weight of a nation of black citizens whose hopes he represented, remains one of the most courageous acts in the long history of civil rights.

Dodgers general manager Branch Rickey knew that the man chosen to play this role had to be someone special. He found such a person in Robinson, a Georgia native who had become a football and track star at UCLA. During a stint in the army during World War II after college, Robinson faced down discrimination from officials in the military with the same calm determination that he

◄ Jackie Robinson's game jersey with its famous No. 42. The jersey is accompanied here by a baseball autographed by Robinson.

◀ This original painting by Yuri Liaboh features Negro League stars Satchel Paige, Josh Gibson, Roy Campanella (later Robinson's Dodgers teammate), and Buck Leonard. In the center is the famous scene of Branch Rickey signing Robinson to a contract.

would later use to succeed in both baseball and in life.

Rickey signed Robinson out of the Negro Leagues after determining that the young man was, as the famous quote goes, "strong enough not to fight back." After a season in the minors, Robinson joined the Dodgers in 1947.

Robinson was not only a pioneer in race relations, a gentleman of the highest order, and a courageous defender of human rights, but he was also an incredible ballplayer. His speed and daring on the base paths has only rarely been matched—he stole home a remarkable 19 times—and his ability to unnerve a pitcher was crucial to many Dodger rallies. He was the 1947 Rookie of the Year, the 1949 MVP, hit .300 or better in six seasons, and helped the Dodgers to six N.L. pennants. His and the team's success was capped off by the "Wait 'til Next Year" 1955 World Series championship.

In 1997, 50 years after that era-defining day and in honor of his importance to baseball, Robinson's No. 42 was officially retired by baseball for all teams. Just as there will never be another Jackie Robinson, no one will ever wear that number again.

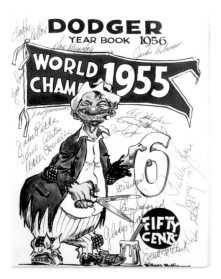

▲ This signed program from the 1956 season features the famous Brooklyn "Bum" celebrating the Dodgers' 1955 title. Robinson's signature can be seen above "1955."

▼ This photo shows Robinson wearing the hat shown below. In 1946, before joining Brooklyn, he first played for the Dodgers' top minor league club, the Montreal Royals. Team executives believed that kinder racial attitudes in Canada would help ease the young man into the difficult times he woud face in the United States.

Satchel Paige

▲ This poster advertised a game between Satchel Paige's Kansas City Monarchs and the Harlem Stars to be played in Indianapolis.

Few players have enjoyed their time on the baseball diamond—or in life—as much as Leroy "Satchel" Paige. The seemingly ageless pitcher with a rocket arm and a bewildering array of pitches was one of the Negro Leagues' most successful and colorful players, and later made a mark on the major leagues at an age when most players are working on their golf games.

A native of Alabama, he earned his famous nickname from a childhood job carrying suitcases at local train stations. After first playing pro ball in the rollicking world of southern black teams, he joined the Negro Leagues' Pittsburgh Crawfords in 1931, where he teamed with Josh Gibson to help create one of the most powerful teams ever.

Paige was a star in the Negro Leagues for 15 years, and baffled white stars in exhibitions as well. In 1934 he matched up against Dizzy Dean when Dean was in his prime, and won 1-0 in 13 innings, with 17 strikeouts.

"Paige was the best pitcher I ever saw," Bob Feller once said. Paige mesmerized hitters with his inimitable "hesitation" pitch; he dazzled them with a fastball so good that in exhibitions he would often tell his fielders to sit down . . . and then strike out the side; and he perfected a curveball he

Immortal Encounter

On July 9, 1978, I visited Satchel Paige in Kansas City. When I arrived at his residence, he and his wife, LaHoma, greeted me like we were lifelong friends. We spent the next three hours talking about baseball, a cherished memory which I recorded on tape. He told me how he got the name Satchel and discussed his career in the Negro Leagues. Satch considered Stan Musial, Ted Williams, and Buck Leonard to be excellent hitters, but he said the greatest hitter of all time was Josh Gibson. He related this story.

"Josh and I played together in the Winter Leagues in Puerto Rico. One day, Josh came out to the mound and said, 'Satch, you strike out all of these bums, but one day I'll be batting against you and we will see how good you really are.' Two years later we were playing in the Negro League All-Star game in Josh's hometown of Pittsburgh. In the eighth inning Josh came to bat with his team down two runs and two runners on base. I reminded him what he said in Puerto Rico and proceeded to throw three pitches by him before he ever moved the bat off his shoulder."

When I asked Satchel about obtaining some mementos from his career, he went up to the attic and brought down his Satchel Paige Touring All-Stars uniform, Cleveland Indians uniform, baseball spikes, and two gloves he used during his career. My visit with Satchel was truly one of the most rewarding experiences of my life.

—Joel Platt

called the "be" ball. Why be ball? "Because it be where I want it to be," he supposedly said.

Paige's way with a phrase became as celebrated as his way with a pitch. His rules for a long life include the famous line, "Don't look back; something might be gaining on you."

He put his rules into practice in 1948 when Cleveland Indians owner Bill Veeck signed Satch to the majors. Thought at first to be a publicity stunt, the old hurler proved he had some juice left, going 6–1 and helping the Indians win the A.L. pennant. He played for Veeck and the St. Louis Browns 1951–1953, saving 21 games. Paige also returned to the majors in 1965 for an admitted stunt with the Kansas City Athletics, though with three scoreless innings against the Red Sox, it proved to be more than just for laughs.

But laughs were what many people got from being around the voluble, entertaining pitcher. Barred from playing in the majors in his prime, he had the last laugh in 1971 when he became the first former Negro League player elected to the Hall of Fame by a special committee. Before his death in 1982, he could look back on a wonderful career and know that no one would ever catch him.

▲ Paige signed this ball to Sports Immortals and donated it along with this autographed, game-used glove and other memorabilia.

▲ These two signed Paige jerseys show two different parts of his long career. The All Stars were one of several winter exhibition teams the entertaining hurler led on nationwide barnstorming tours. The Indians jersey is from his all-too-brief stint in Cleveland, when he went 6–1 in his "rookie" year of 1948 at age 42. Both jerseys, along with his game-used baseball spikes, are autographed by Paige for Sports Immortals.

Ted Williams

▲ Sports artist Robert Stephen Simon created this painting depicting more than 40 years of Boston Red Sox superstars. Ted Williams (left) patrolled left field for Boston from 1939–1960. Carl Yastrzemski (right) took over for Williams in 1961 and was the 1967 MVP while becoming the last player to win the Triple Crown. Both Hall of Fame players signed this unique piece of artwork.

Growing up in San Diego, Ted Williams set his sights early on becoming "the greatest hitter who ever lived." In a marvelous 21-year career with the Boston Red Sox, he probably achieved that goal. He posted a lifetime .344 average, won two Most Valuable Player awards (and probably should have won five), led the A.L. in home runs and RBI five times, and more than any other player applied both art and science to the study of hitting a baseball.

Perhaps his greatest hitting achievement came in 1941, only his third season in the big leagues. Williams had quickly become one of baseball's top hitters, but he really put his name in lights in 1941. He was hitting .430 in mid-May and never stopped his blazing pace, even as the baseball world paid more attention to Joe DiMaggio's 56-game hitting streak that summer. DiMaggio's streak ended, but Williams kept hitting.

Entering the final day of the season, a double-header against the Athletics, Williams was hitting .39955. That would have rounded up to .400 in the record books and made him the first player since Bill Terry in 1931 to reach that hallowed mark. He could have sat out the game and sealed it. It was a mark of Williams' stubborn nature and desire to be nothing but the best, that he went out and risked falling below .400. It wasn't much of a risk, however, and he had six hits in eight at-bats, finally reaching a season average of .406. No player since has topped .400.

Soon after, Williams turned his keen eye away from fastballs and onto runways. He enlisted in the marines in 1942 and became a pilot. To serve his country, he gave up three of the prime years of his baseball career. In 1952 he did it again, spending two years as one of the marines' top jet pilots and surviving a crash landing.

After returning to the Red Sox following World War II, he picked up where he left off, winning the 1946 A.L. MVP and leading the Red Sox to the World Series. He won the 1947 Triple Crown, and led the Sox achingly close to more Series in 1948 and 1949. The championship eluded Williams and Boston throughout his career, but his outstanding hitting skills went on undiminished. He won a batting title at the age of 38 in 1958, batting .388. And in 1960, in his final at-bat, he hit a home run.

After his illustrious career, Williams, already a success as a hitter and pilot, became one of the world's greatest fly-fishermen. He is the only person to be selected to both the fishing and baseball Halls of Fame.

To top it all off, Williams has become, in his old age, baseball's beloved elder statesman. The cantankerous and stubborn hitter who battled the press and refused to tip his cap to the fans was lauded by all of baseball when he was named to the All-Century Team in 1999.

How many of us can say that our lifelong goals were achieved? That the dreams we had as children came true? The man they called "Teddy Ballgame" can look back and know that when he goes down the street, people do indeed say: There goes the greatest hitter who ever lived.

▲ Ted Williams' famous number 9 Boston Red Sox game uniform.

Rip Sewell
837 Russell Drive
Plant City, Florida 33566
Aug 30/78

TO THE SPORTS IMMORTALS MUSEUM:
ONE OF THE MOST SIGNIFICANT MOMENTS
IN MY SPORTS CAREER HAPPENED IN 1946
IN THE ALL-STAR GAME AT FENWAY PARK IN
BOSTON TED WILLIAMS THE ONLY PLAYER TO
HIT MY BLOOPER PITCH FOR A HOME RUN,
IT WAS A TWO BALL AND TWO STRIKE COUNT
THE TRUE STORY THAT HAS NEVER BEEN TOLD
BEFORE WAS THAT TED WILLIAMS IN ORDER TO
HIT THE BLOOPER HAD TAKEN TWO STEPS FORWARD
AND WAS OUT OF THE BATTERS BOX AND WOULD
HAVE BEEN CALLED OUT BY HOME PLATE UMPIRE
LARRY GOETZ IF IT WAS A REGULAR SEASON
GAME.

Sincerely,
Rip Sewell

◄ In this letter to Sports Immortals, pitcher Rip Sewell tells his side of the home run Williams hit in the 1946 All-Star Game. Williams sent Sewell's famous "eephus" blooper into the Fenway Park seats, but Sewell claims here that Williams was "out of the batter's box and would have been called out . . . if it was a regular season game."

Roberto Clemente

It is the rare athlete whose influence can still be felt every time players in his sport take the field, but that is certainly the case with Roberto Clemente. The first great Latin superstar in baseball, he influenced generations of Hispanic players since and helped turn baseball into a truly international sport.

But Clemente's impact on the world extends far beyond the playing field. Few athletes were as concerned with others as was Clemente, who made helping children and the less fortunate, both in the United States and in his native Puerto Rico, a primary component of his life.

Growing up in a small farming town where young players used sticks for bats and rolled-up socks for baseballs, he showed enough talent to play professionally in his teens. After starring for the Santurce Cangrejeros (Crabbers), he was lured north by the Pittsburgh Pirates.

Young Clemente, though obviously skilled, started his career slowly, and didn't really blossom until 1960, his sixth season, when he batted .314 and led the N.L. with 19 assists, the latter courtesy of a throwing arm still considered among the greatest ever. More importantly, Clemente helped the Pirates win their first World Series since 1925. In 1961 he became the first Hispanic player to win the batting title; his .351 average was the second of 13 consecutive .300 seasons. He was also the 1966 MVP, and for the rest of the decade was among the game's great stars, both offensively and defensively. Meanwhile he continued to raise funds and awareness for children's programs in Pittsburgh and Puerto Rico.

In 1971 Clemente led the Pirates to the World Series once again. More than 20 years after he had left the sugarcane fields behind to star in the majors, he made the most of this chance at center stage. He batted .414, hit two homers, and made several stunning defensive plays. He was named

▲ The year 2001 saw the bobble head doll return to popularity. This rare older model of Clemente is the most valuable.

▼ Clemente wore this cap during his 21-year Hall of Fame career with the Pirates. The hat is autographed on the brim.

▲ The thank you letter above, signed by Clemente, commemorates a day held in his honor in 1970.

the MVP of the Series that Pittsburgh won in seven games over the Orioles.

Just three months after getting his 3,000th hit on the final day of the 1972 season, Clemente boarded a plane on its way to a disaster site in Nicaragua. Following an earthquake there, he had quickly rallied support for the victims and relief supplies were sent from Puerto Rico to Managua. But Clemente learned that some of the aid wasn't getting through, and decided to go personally to make sure the supplies were delivered. His selfless gesture was his last; the plane carrying Clemente and four others crashed on takeoff on December 31, 1972. A hero had died.

Today, Major League Baseball calls its highest honor for community service the Roberto Clemente Award; many players consider winning it a greater reward than all the MVPs in the world.

▲ The sleeveless jersey Clemente wore in 1962 and another jersey worn in the 1971 World Series when he was named MVP. Also, a signed, game-used bat is shown with an autographed ball.

Immortal Encounter

In my opinion, Roberto Clemente was the most outstanding baseball player of all time. He could run, hit, field, and throw like very few others. When the baseball left his arm in right field, it was as if it was shot out of a cannon. He was, without a doubt, one of my favorite athletes.

I spent a lot of time with my hero in Pittsburgh during the 1960s. We became very friendly, and every time we saw each other at the ballpark (Forbes Field and later Three Rivers Stadium), Roberto asked about the Sports Immortals Museum.

In 1971 Roberto told me about his plans for a Sports City in Puerto Rico, and he asked me if I would help him with a museum. I told him I would be glad to assist. However, tragedy struck a year later on New

Year's Eve. Roberto took off on a plane from Puerto Rico with a cargo full of food and supplies on a relief mission to aid victims of a massive earthquake in Managua, Nicaragua. Unfortunately, the plane crashed shortly after takeoff and Roberto was dead at 38.

Over the course of our many encounters, Roberto gave me several game-used bats and autographed baseballs. He also told Joe O'Toole, then the vice president of the Pittsburgh Pirates, to send me his uniform from the 1962 season, along with the uniform he wore when he was named the most valuable player of the 1971 World Series.

I'm proud to include these mementos in the Sports Immortals collection.

—JOEL PLATT

Cal Ripken Jr.

▲ This artistic celebration of Ripken's monumental feat was created for Sports Immortals by artist Robert Stephen Simon.

For more than 50 years, the number 2,130 was instantly recognizable by baseball fans as shorthand for consistency, devotion, doggedness, and excellence. That number represented the consecutive-games-played streak put together by Lou Gehrig from 1925–1939.

As of September 6, 1995, sports fans everywhere learned that they would have to learn a new number when Orioles shortstop Cal Ripken Jr. played his 2,131st game in a row. Ripken's streak, incredibly, would continue for 501 more games before he finally ended it voluntarily in 1998 at 2,632 games. The record many said would never be broken was not just broken; it was demolished.

As Ripken took a victory lap around Oriole Park at Camden Yards, fans cheered for more than 20 minutes, while a nationwide TV audience watched in awe. The record set by a great player and a great man had been broken; how fitting that it was broken by another person who combined talent on the field with compassion and humility off it.

Ripken certainly worked hard to earn that record, playing through hurts both major and minor, and through slumps short and long. But he was more than just a steady name in the lineup; he was nearly always one of the best players.

Ripken broke into the majors in 1982 and quickly went right to the top, winning rookie of the year honors; in his second season, he was the MVP and helped the Orioles win the title. He was MVP again in 1991 while continuing a string of

▲ This is one of Ripken's game-used gloves.

Baseball

▲ Along with a Ripken game-used jersey, this display features a signed bat from his 1982 Rookie of the Year season, an autographed baseball, and a signed ticket and program from his last game on October 6, 2001.

All-Star Game appearances that would finally total 19 at his retirement in 2001. Recognized as an outstanding hitter, he also was a top fielder, winning a pair of Gold Gloves. His many talents proved to the next generation that height and strength and the shortstop position are not mutually exclusive. He set a new standard for young, superstar shortstops such as Alex Rodriguez, Nomar Garciaparra, and Derek Jeter.

Ripken also built a reputation as one of baseball's nicest guys, one who was always ready with an autograph or a helping hand. Among his many community service honors was the Roberto Clemente Award in 1992.

But even with his many other achievements, Ripken's singular and memorable number of 2,632 will remain his most lasting impact on the game.

Basketball

▲ Clockwise from top left: Maurice Stokes varsity sweater; Bill Russell Celtics rookie card and jersey; Houston Comets championship ball; Jerry West game jersey; Bob Lanier game-used sneaker; Pete Maravich college game jersey; early pro basketball poster; USA "Dream Team" autographed photo; 1896 ball signed by Dolph Schayes; Bob Cousy autographed All-Star jersey; Elgin Baylor game jersey.

Immortals Who Inspire

Here are stories of athletes whose achievement of character exceeded their achievements of skill.

Magic Johnson

We remember Earvin "Magic" Johnson for the Cheshire-cat grin that belied his fierce intensity. We remember him for his three NBA MVP awards and 12 All-Star selections. We remember him as a 20-year-old rookie who moved from point guard to center to replace the injured Kareem Abdul-Jabbar in the 1980 NBA Finals and led the Lakers to a title-clinching victory. And we remember him for his legendary duels with rival Larry Bird, first in the 1979 NCAA Final, then again when either Johnson's Lakers or Bird's Celtics—or both—vied for the NBA title.

But Magic Johnson's greatest battle wasn't on the hardwood. Instead, it officially started on November 7, 1991, when he tearfully announced his retirement from competitive basketball at 32 because he had tested positive for HIV—the virus that causes AIDS.

The news shocked not only the basketball community but also the world, which had embraced Johnson as a beloved ambassador whose enthusiasm and personal appeal transcended sports.

At the time, the announcement seemed like a death sentence. Indeed, AIDS-related deaths were growing at an alarming rate in the United States and throughout much of the world. But more than a decade later, Johnson is as vibrant and as active as ever.

A planned comeback to the NBA was cut short in 1992 amid unwarranted health concerns expressed by other players, and another comeback in 1996 lasted only 32 games. But Johnson remains in peak physical condition, a tribute to an unrelenting diet and exercise regimen, and to dramatic strides in the treatment of the virus.

Johnson helped lead the United States to the gold medal at the 1992 Olympics and annually appears in charity basketball games. Off the court, he has established himself as a pillar in the business community, attacking his pursuits with the same voracity and applying the same work ethic that made him a success in his athletic endeavors.

Johnson's business empire includes shopping malls, restaurants, and coffee shops, a bank, a record label, physical-fitness facilities, and much more. More important, his success has provided inspiration and hope to thousands of other people throughout the world afflicted with the AIDS virus. The strength, courage, and character that he showed while making "Magic" on the court became his weapons in the biggest fight of all— for his life.

▲ This signed, game-used Magic Johnson rookie jersey features one of the most famous numbers in sports.

Michael Jordan

It was Father's Day, 1996, and the Chicago Bulls had just wrapped up the NBA title with an 87–75 victory over the Seattle SuperSonics. And Michael Jordan wept.

He wept for the joy of winning his fourth NBA title, just two seasons removed from a self-imposed retirement that kept him out of basketball during the 1993–1994 season. And he wept for the memory of his own father, James Jordan, who had been murdered in North Carolina in the summer of 1993.

Michael Jordan called James Jordan "my best friend." James Jordan was there to hug his son when he led the Bulls to the first of three consecutive NBA titles in 1991. And father was there to hug son when the Bulls concluded their remarkable run by winning the title on Father's Day, 1993. The younger Jordan had just won his seventh consecutive NBA scoring title that season, a feat previously accomplished only by the legendary Wilt Chamberlain. He was on top of the world, a superstar celebrity whose appeal extended even to those who didn't know the difference between a basketball and a bowling ball. Corporate America was in love with him as a pitchman whose popularity knew no bounds, crossing boundaries of gender, race, and geography.

But just one month later, Michael Jordan was shattered by the news that his father had been murdered in North Carolina by thieves after he stopped to rest on the roadside. James Jordan's body was found in a South Carolina creek nearly two weeks after he last had been seen alive.

The loss had such a devastating effect on the basketball star that it contributed greatly to his decision to retire before the 1993–1994 season and spend more time with his own family. One year later, he returned—and he nearly led the Bulls back to the 1995 NBA Finals.

By June of 1996, they were back. Chicago won a record 70 games during the regular season, and won the first three games of the NBA Finals against Seattle, dropped the next two, then came home for the Father's Day clincher. Jordan dedicated the game to his father.

"Deep down inside, [my mind] was geared to what was most important to me," Jordan said after scoring 22 points to go along with nine rebounds, seven assists, and two steals. "[That] was my family and my father not being here to see this."

And so he wept.

"Dad's still my hero," Jordan said years after his father's death, "and always will be."

As much for his courage and ability to persevere as for his awesome basketball skills, millions of fans around the world feel the the same way about Jordan.

▲ The great Michael Jordan signed his rookie-season Chicago Bulls jersey for Sports Immortals.

George Mikan

▲ Mikan sent this letter to Sports Immortals after Joel Platt asked the former Lakers star to name the five greatest players of all time. Writing in 1999, Mikan named, in order, Wilt Chamberlain, Bob Cousy, Michael Jordan, Bob Pettit, and Bill Russell. He might have had a good case to include himself on that list.

Basketball was invented to be played on the ground. Sure, the basket was 10 feet above the gym floor, but the ground was where the players remained for the most part. The early game was one of passing, little dribbling, and set shots. Tall guys were not valued, since they usually moved like they were on stilts.

In the 1930s, players started jumping, moving more quickly, and coming up with a wide variety of shots. But still, the tallest players were not the stars.

Then along came a bespectacled string bean named George Mikan and basketball was forever after played among the tall trees.

Mikan first became a star in college at DePaul. The 6'10" center was the first big man with the ability to move with grace, speed, and timing. His array of shots and his overpowering presence on defense almost literally reinvented the game. A three-time All-America and two-time national scoring champion, he led DePaul to the 1945 NIT title (in the days when that was the tournament to win).

The NBA wasn't even around when Mikan wanted to turn pro, but its predecessor, the National Basketball League, quickly snapped him up, and he led the Chicago Gears to the title. He repeated the championship with the Minneapolis Lakers the next season. In 1949 the NBA was formed by the merger of the NBL and another pro league. Soon Mikan was dominating that league, too.

Led by Mikan's unstoppable hook shot, his lane-hogging defense, and his innovative passing, the Lakers put together the NBA's first dynasty, winning five titles in six seasons.

▲ Mikan is fifth from the right, the player wearing eyeglasses, in this autographed team photo of the 1953–1954 Minneapolis Lakers.

Basketball

Mikan was so good that Madison Square Garden once put up a sign that read simply: "Tonight: Geo. Mikan vs. Knicks." His career average of 23.1 points per game is still among the all-time top 20, which is amazing considering all the great players who have followed him. He was named to the Basketball Hall of Fame and was one of the only players from the early NBA named to the league's Top 50 team in 1999.

Mikan retired after the 1954 season (though he had a brief, Jordan-like comeback), and was later briefly the Lakers' coach and the commissioner of the American Basketball Association. He now lives in Arizona after a long career as a lawyer.

While big men like Shaquille O'Neal, Kareem Abdul-Jabbar, Wilt Chamberlain, and others have earned glory as dominating centers, all of them must point to George Mikan as the player who showed them that the best way to the top was to be closer to the top to begin with.

Immortal Encounter

On July 18, 1978, I flew to Minneapolis seeking memorabilia from basketball legend George Mikan. We had spoken several times on the phone and arranged a meeting. I spent two hours interviewing him at his home about his basketball career.

George said that the athlete he most admired growing up was Babe Ruth. The person who had the greatest influence on developing his basketball skills was his coach at DePaul, Ray Meyer. I asked him who he thought was the greatest basketball player of all time, and he said Wilt Chamberlain.

I thought Mikan was one of the most articulate athletes I had ever met. We took several photos together and as I was about to leave, George gave me his complete uniform and warm-up suit that he wore while winning championships with the Minneapolis Lakers.

—JOEL PLATT

Wilt Chamberlain

The numbers put up by Wilt Chamberlain are staggering just by themselves. Seven NBA scoring titles, including one season (1961–1962) in which he averaged—averaged!—50.4 points per game. Seven seasons in a row in which he averaged more than 40 ppg. Scoring more than 60 points in a game 32 times, 50 or more points in 118 games, and more than 40 in 271 games. He blew away the previous single-game scoring record with 78 points in 1962. Then he topped that himself by scoring 100 points in a game later that season.

But the attitude with which Wilt Chamberlain put those numbers up is just as big a part of his story. He simply would not let himself be stopped. He scored and scored and scored. He had a will for the basket almost unmatched in NBA history. Remarkably, he also never fouled out of an NBA game, a stat that would be virtually impossible to achieve in basketball today.

Growing up in Philadelphia, the "Stilt" scored as many as 70 points per game three times in high school, once scoring 60 points in only 12 minutes. He earned another of his many nicknames, the "Big Dipper," after he had to dip his head under some low pipes in his school building. In college

▲ Chamberlain's signature is below this poster advertising the world-famous Harlem Globetrotters, for whom he played after leaving Kansas and before joining the NBA.

▲ Chamberlain autographed these three jerseys tracing the arc of his career: at bottom right, his Overbrook High jersey from Philadelphia; at top, from the Warriors 1966–1967 season; at bottom left, his 1971–1972 Lakers jersey.

Basketball

he set a school record at the University of Kansas with 53 points, and later led Kansas to the national title game.

Joining the NBA in 1959, the 7'2" Chamberlain was named the NBA MVP and Rookie of the Year while leading the league with a 37.6 ppg average. He won the next six scoring titles in a row, a feat later matched only by Michael Jordan.

Wilt's scoring totals reached their height with his incredible 100-point performance on March 2, 1962, in Hershey, Pennsylvania. Early in the game, Wilt's Philadelphia Warriors teammates knew that the Stilt was hot and kept feeding him the ball. As the game went on, the shots continued to pour in from every angle. Chamberlain, never a good free-throw shooter, even made a career-best 28 of 32 free-throw attempts. In the end, Chamberlain scored his 100th point on a dunk with just 42 seconds remaining in the game. There are many records in the NBA that are potentially unreachable; most experts agree that Wilt's single-game record is right at the top of that list.

Chamberlain played until 1973, helping the Warriors win the title in 1966–1967, and the Lakers win it all in 1971–1972. He was the NBA's all-time leading scorer and rebounder when he retired and more than 30 years later, he's still among the top five in scoring. The Stilt still stands tall among NBA legends.

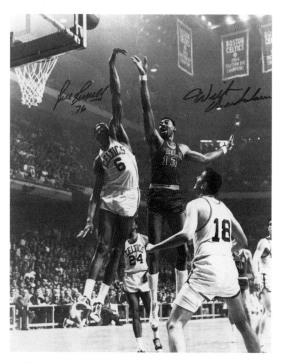

▲ The head-to-head battles between legendary Boston Celtics center Bill Russell (No. 6) and Chamberlain (No. 13)—both of whom signed this photo—were NBA showstoppers throughout the 1960s.

Immortal Encounter

In the late '50s I decided to take a trip to Philadelphia to obtain some mementos from Wilt Chamberlain, the basketball phenom who starred at Overbrook High School and the University of Kansas. The Chamberlain house was located in the Overbrook section of Philadelphia. When I knocked on the front door, I was greeted by Wilt's mother and sister. They invited me in, but were sorry to inform me that Wilt had gone back to the university earlier that day. I told them about my goal to establish a museum to honor sports immortals. They presented me Wilt's Overbrook High School uniform that had just been retired. They said they were sure that Wilt would be proud to have his uniform in the Sports Immortals Collection.

Several years later, I obtained Wilt's Philadelphia and Los Angeles uniforms from his championship years with both teams.

In the 1990s, Wilt opened the Wilt Chamberlain Restaurant in Boca Raton, Florida. My daughter Wendy and I met with Wilt at the restaurant and he autographed all three uniforms. Touching the uniforms, he said, "This is like reliving my entire basketball career."

—JOEL PLATT

Oscar Robertson

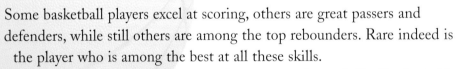

Some basketball players excel at scoring, others are great passers and defenders, while still others are among the top rebounders. Rare indeed is the player who is among the best at all these skills.

Oscar Robertson, however, performed all of basketball's many skills at the highest level; few players before or since match Robertson for all-around mastery of the sport. How good was the "Big O"? In 1961–1962, before the term "triple-double" was even invented, he posted double-figure averages for the *season* in scoring, assists, and rebounding. No one else has ever done that.

If Robertson had stopped playing before he got to the NBA, he would still be a legend for his deeds in high school, college, and the Olympics.

At Crispus Attucks High School in Indiana, he was a three-time all-state player, but more importantly, he led the school to the first state championship ever won by a predominantly African-American school.

At the University of Cincinnati, Robertson quickly moved the Bearcats into the NCAA's top ranks. He was a three-time national player of the year and scoring champion, and helped Cincinnati earn two Final Four berths. His 2,973 career points are still among the all-time top 10. (In honor of his college success, the Basketball Writers Association annually awards the Oscar Robertson Trophy to its player of the year.) In 1960, following his final college season, he led the U.S. Olympic team to a gold medal at the Summer Games in Rome.

In the NBA, with the Cincinnati Royals, Robertson wasted little time in continuing his all-around success, being named All-Star Game MVP and Rookie of the Year. In 1961–1962, he averaged 30.8 points, 11.4 assists, and 12.5 rebounds per game. Many players since have "doubled" in a pair of categories, but none has gone triple-double for an entire season.

After moving to the Milwaukee Bucks, Robertson teamed with a young Lew Alcindor (later Kareem Abdul-Jabbar) to win his only NBA championship in 1971.

▲ Robertson wasted little time succeeding in the NBA while wearing this Cincinnati Royals uniform; he was the 1961 rookie of the year and the All-Star Game MVP.

Not only did he have a major influence on how the game was played, Robertson played a big part in how the game was run, serving as president of the NBA Players' Association for 10 years and helping the league introduce free agency.

Robertson, called the "most versatile player I've ever seen" by coaching legend Red Auerbach, retired as the NBA's all-time leader in assists and free throws made, but more importantly, he left an inspiring legacy of versatility and all-around success that players are still trying to emulate.

▲ You know you're a superstar when you get a letter all to yourself. There is only one "Big 0," as shown on his Milwaukee Bucks warm-up suit.

▲ This signed Robertson sneaker shows just how far the sport's footwear has come in the decades since he played. He also signed the ball with which he made such magic.

Bill Walton & Maurice Lucas

Portland, Oregon, has never made much of a mark on the national sports scene. The lovely and pleasant Northwest city has never had a major league baseball or NFL team or hosted a major bowl game.

But in 1977 the city was home to the NBA champions, an unexpectedly dominant Trailblazers team led by a pair of veteran warriors, Bill Walton and Maurice Lucas.

Walton had, of course, already enjoyed massive success while in college, helping UCLA win two NCAA titles and earning for himself two player of the year awards and two Final Four MVP trophies. His 44-point, 21-for-22 performance in the 1973 title game is still among the tournament's greatest individual performances.

The laidback San Diego native, a famous fan of the Grateful Dead, was not a prototypical center. Instead, Walton excelled at passing, defense, and possessed a soft scoring touch, rather than the intimidating inside presence that most big men had.

Meanwhile, after displaying his warrior stance at Marquette for three years, Lucas joined the ABA after his junior year. He was a tough inside player whose role in the NBA helped define the modern power forward position. Said Lucas' Portland teammate Lionel Hollins, "To Lucas, basketball was a contact sport." Lucas always gave 100 percent effort and played every game with intense emotion.

But in Lucas, Walton found the perfect mate. The Trail Blazers had finished dead last in 1975–1976 and knew they

▼ Maurice Lucas went from the Pittsburgh playgrounds—including Joel Platt's backyard court—to the NBA. He signed this 1977 Blazers team ball to Joel in appreciation.

▲ Walton wore this uniform and shoes while winning his only world title. Presaging the nagging injuries that would hamper his career, he also wore the foot wrapping shown at center in the 1977 NBA finals.

needed a powerful player inside to complement Walton. They got him in Lucas, and together the pair helped finally put Portland on the sports map.

In the NBA Finals, the Blazers were matched up against the heavily favored and high-scoring Philadelphia 76ers. No one was surprised when Portland lost the first two games. But the team regrouped and Lucas stepped up defensive pressure on Philly's George McGinnis and Darryl Dawkins, and Walton found room to score. For only the second time in NBA history, a team came back from two games behind to win the championship.

To show how important the two players jointly were to Portland, the following season they started 50–10, but after Walton was injured, Portland collapsed and lost in the first round of the playoffs.

Walton would go on to be named NBA MVP in 1978 and win the Sixth Man Award in 1986, but injuries would eventually curtail what many feel would have been an all-time great career. Pittsburgh native Lucas continued his tough-guy play for several teams until retiring after a solid 14-year career in 1988. Separately, neither player had reached the top. But by combining forces, by sharing their talents, they lifted their team to the championship.

▲ Lucas donated this uniform, worn while winning the NBA championship, to the Sports Immortals collection, with thanks to his old friend from Pittsburgh, Joel Platt.

Immortal Encounter

During his career he was one of the NBA's premier power forwards. Affectionately referred to as the "Enforcer," Maurice Lucas took the court with a warrior mentality and the heart of a lion.

I met Maurice during his senior year at Schenly High School in Pittsburgh. Our friendship was cemented forever when I loaned him my car to take his girlfriend to the school prom. During his college career, Maurice would often visit my home and study the rules on my basketball court which read, "No Smoking, No Drinking,

No Drugs! Practice and Dedication Bring Success."

Our relationship over the years has been one of great respect and mutual admiration. To me, Maurice Lucas is a very special person. He has combined great determination, God-given athletic ability, and the academic principles taught by his mother to achieve success on the basketball court and as a business entrepreneur. I'm also grateful that he contributed one of the Forewords to this book.

—JOEL PLATT

Kareem Abdul-Jabbar

What's in a name? In the case of Kareem Abdul-Jabbar, everything. His name means "noble, powerful servant" in Arabic. Possessing a grace and calm that belied his size, a devastating sky hook, and an ability to mesh his skills with his team's to achieve victory, the man who was born Lew Alcindor lived up to his new appellation. Abdul-Jabbar won six NBA MVP awards, played in a record 18 All-Star Games, and became the NBA's all-time leading scorer. He helped his teams win a total of six NBA titles.

After crushing opponents in New York high school basketball, the young Alcindor helped UCLA win three NCAA championships. Joining the Milwaukee Bucks in 1969, he averaged 28.8 points per game as a rookie.

After winning a scoring title and helping Milwaukee win an NBA title in 1971, the same year he changed his name, Abdul-Jabbar left the Bucks and joined the Los Angeles Lakers in 1975. In 1979, after Magic Johnson joined

▲ Abdul-Jabbar wore this uniform and these protective goggles while helping the Lakers win five titles.

▼ Then–Lew Alcindor wore these low-tech sneakers in the 1970 NBA All-Star Game. He autographed them after the game and gave them to Sports Immortals.

Immortal Encounter

My first encounter with Adbul-Jabbar was at the NBA All-Star Game in Philadelphia in 1970. I met him in the locker room prior to the game and told him about the museum collection. He said if I would meet him at the Marriott Hotel after the game he would give me the shoes he used that night. Once the game was over, I drove through a heavy snowstorm to get to the hotel before the team arrived. When I got there, the players were checking in at the front desk. Lew was talking to some friends when he saw me coming through the front entrance with two inches of snow dripping from my raincoat. He immediately went over to his duffel bag and retrieved the

pair of sneakers he had just worn in the All-Star game.

"Joel," he said, "you deserve these shoes. I never thought you would make it through the storm." He autographed the shoes (above) and said to keep him informed on the development of the museum.

Several years later I met him during a pregame Los Angeles Lakers practice. We reminisced about that winter day in Philadelphia. Just then, Magic Johnson, then the Lakers' prized rookie, walked by and Kareem introduced us. At the conclusion of the game, I was able to secure the game jerseys that Kareem and Magic wore that night. —JOEL PLATT

Basketball

the team, the duo led the Lakers to five NBA titles in the 1980s. With Abdul-Jabbar's high scoring and shot-blocking and Magic's adept orchestration of the "Showtime" offense, the Lakers were the best team of the decade.

Throughout his long career, Abdul-Jabbar kept himself in excellent shape, and was very agile for someone so tall (7'2"). His greatest weapon was the mighty sky hook, which he developed in high school and college against much smaller opponents. He quickly found that it still worked against the pros, too. From anywhere inside 18 feet or so, the shot was deadly and impossible to stop.

Abdul-Jabbar's scoring feats are stunning: he scored 10 or more points in 787 straight games. He scored nearly 5,000 points more than the second all-time leading scorer, Karl Malone. He averaged 20 points or more every season from 1969–1986. In 1984 he scored his 31,420th point, overtaking Wilt Chamberlain to become the leading scorer in NBA history. The "Big Fella" was at the top of the charts, and he remains there today with an incredible 38,387 career points.

▲ The Milwaukee Bucks were Abdul-Jabbar's first stop on the road to superstardom. The Bucks chose him to wear this uniform (and warm-up pants) with the first pick in the 1969 NBA Draft.

Abdul-Jabbar wore this UCLA Bruins warm-up jacket when he was still known as Lew Alcindor.

Shaquille O'Neal

There are big men, and there are BIG men. Shaquille O'Neal is the latter, thundering down the court at 7'1" and 335 pounds. He is perhaps the most athletic and multitalented big man in NBA history. Off the court, he is shy, quiet, and a huge hit with kids, but on the court he has become basketball's unstoppable force.

Twice a scoring champion, the man they call "Shaq Daddy" is always among league leaders in scoring (including finishing second three times), while regularly posting high field-goal accuracy marks. A star from his first NBA game, when he grabbed 18 rebounds, O'Neal quickly became a dominating force inside for the Orlando Magic. He was the NBA Rookie of the Year for 1992–1993, and nearly won his first scoring title the next year, losing out to David Robinson on the final day of the season.

In the 1993–1994 season, young Shaq took the Magic all the way to the NBA Finals, while winning his first scoring title with a 29.3 average. After moving to the Los Angeles Lakers for the 1996–1997 season, O'Neal continued his high-scoring ways, averaging 26.2 points. In fact, he has never averaged less than 26 points per game in a season since his rookie year, and his per-game average was third all-time entering the 2001–2002 season.

▼ Shaq signed this original painted ball by Yuri Liaboh when he was with the Orlando Magic, early in his great career.

▲ O'Neal's game-worn jersey from the Lakers' 2001 championship season. Shaq's No. 34 should one day join the Lakers' seven other retired numbers.

Basketball

For all of O'Neal's monster slams, hit rap albums, and movie and TV appearances, his finest hours came at the end of the 1999–2000 season, when he and Kobe Bryant led the Lakers to the NBA's best record. O'Neal not only won his second scoring title by averaging 29.7 ppg, but he dominated in the postseason, averaging 38 points per game in the NBA finals against Indiana. The Lakers won their first NBA title with O'Neal at center, and he was named Finals MVP to go along with his season MVP award. The title and the award seemed to validate O'Neal's talent, as he took the great leap forward from high-scoring center to game-breaking superstar.

The Lakers and Shaq made it two in a row in 2001, putting on one of the most dominating postseason performances in sports history. L.A. lost only one game on its way to capturing the second title of the Shaq Era, while O'Neal himself turned in his second Finals MVP performance. The big man is going to need a big trophy case if he keeps this up.

▲ This is a game-worn autographed O'Neal shoe. He wears an enormous size 22EEE shoe.

▲ Clockwise from top left: shoes worn by Jack Dempsey when he beat Luis Firpo; Evander Holyfield's fight robe; Rocky Marciano autographed gloves from when he knocked out Don Cockell; Roy Jones Jr. signed trunks; 1919 Willard/Dempsey ticket; Fitzsimmons/Jeffries 1902 program; 1923 Tendler/Leonard fight program; pennant from 1921 Dempsey/Carpentier fight; punching bag used by James J. Corbett.

Boxing

▲ This is a ticket from the 1936 bout between Joe Louis and Max Schmeling, while the program is from their 1938 fight at Yankee Stadium.

▼ Harry Greb won this 18-karat gold medal for a victory in his native Pittsburgh. He went on to become world champion in two weight classes.

Immortals Who Inspire

Here are stories of athletes whose achievement of character exceeded their achievements of skill.

Joe Louis

In 1938, American Joe Louis went to war in the boxing ring against German Max Schmeling. Never mind that a real war was looming in Europe over real freedoms, never mind that Schmeling was not a Nazi—the symbolism of the conflict was too great for the international media or the American public to overlook: democracy versus fascism, good versus evil.

Schmeling's native country had just overrun Austria and was threatening much of the surrounding area. And Adolf Hitler personally had taken note of Schmeling's victory over Louis two years earlier—to that date, the only loss in the Brown Bomber's career—calling it proof of Aryan supremacy.

Louis, on the other hand, exemplified the best of American values. He was humble, soft-spoken, and hard-working. As an African-American man fighting in a predominately white man's sport, he had overcome long odds to become the heavyweight champion of the world in 1937 by knocking out incumbent champion James J. Braddock.

Louis was a title-holder who was popular with boxing fans of all ages and races. In subsequent years, he would donate much of his winnings to military relief efforts, and in 1942, he joined the army. While in the service, he fought dozens of exhibitions in morale-boosting efforts at military outposts around the world.

But in New York's Yankee Stadium on June 22, 1938, Louis did a service to his country by pummeling his German nemesis. In an unrelenting 124 seconds, the Brown Bomber avenged his loss to Schmeling and became a symbol of national pride. He knocked his opponent down three times before Schmeling's trainer threw in the towel 56 seconds before the end of the first round.

Harry Greb

Before every fight, boxers meticulously undergo the tale of the tape. They are carefully weighed and closely measured. But there hasn't been an instrument invented that can accurately gauge a man's heart. If there was such a device, it would have found Harry Greb's heart to be among the biggest.

Greb was just 5'8" and 158 pounds. He lost sight in one eye during a match early in his career. The sight in his good eye began failing him late in his career. He was a middleweight who often fought light-heavyweight and heavyweight boxers who were bigger, stronger, and packed a more powerful punch. But the diminutive fighter, who grew up in Pittsburgh at the turn of the 20th century, dreaming that he'd one day become a boxing champion, flourished because of his courage, wits, and a lightning barrage of punches.

Greb's career was as frenzied as those punches, which came so fast and furious that he was known as the "Human Windmill." He fought 299 times between 1913 and 1926, and lost only eight bouts. In 1922 he handed legendary Gene Tunney the lone defeat of his career to win the vacant light-heavyweight title, and a year later, he became the world middleweight champion.

But Greb had a nemesis, and it was fellow middleweight Tiger Flowers. The fighters squared off twice in 1926, with Flowers winning a pair of brutal, 15-round split decisions. The second fight came on August 19 at Madison Square Garden in New York.

Two months later, Greb died of a heart attack following an operation to remove a cataract from his eye. He was just 32.

Sugar Ray Leonard

If ever a sport exemplified survival of the fittest, it's boxing. Not only is the sport so obviously physical in nature, but a boxer has to start at the bottom of the ladder and painstakingly climb to the top rung. Along the way, any number of fighters can knock him back down the ladder.

There are enough built-in obstacles facing any would-be champion. Now add injury, age, and inactivity, and the odds become even greater. And yet that's just what former lightweight and welterweight champion Sugar Ray Leonard had to overcome when he decided to come out of retirement for a second time to fight "Marvelous" Marvin Hagler for the world middleweight title in Las Vegas in 1987.

Leonard was well aware of the uphill battle he faced. He was only 30 years old, not exactly advanced even by athletic standards. However, his opponent was two years younger and in the prime of his career. More importantly, Leonard had not fought in nearly three years. He originally retired in 1982 after suffering a detached retina in his left eye, then came back to win one fight in 1984 before stepping out of the ring again—this time, he thought, for good.

But a fighter's will to win does not disappear so readily, and Leonard was determined to reach the top of the ladder once more. After watching Hagler defend his title in a fight in 1986, Leonard was convinced he could step into the ring with the bigger and stronger champion.

After 12 grueling rounds with Hagler, Leonard nearly collapsed from exhaustion. But even before he was pronounced victorious by decision, Sugar Ray knew he had accomplished his goal.

"I was a winner by going the distance with Marvin," he told ABC's *Wide World of Sports*. "I was a winner by standing up to Marvin. I was a winner by exchanging punches with Marvin. It didn't matter if I got the decision—I did the impossible."

▲ Greb earned this trophy for defeating Tommy Gibbons in 1922 to win the light-heavyweight title; the ticket is from one of his fights against nemesis Tiger Flowers.

▲ Sugar Ray is pictured with Sports Immortals founder Joel Platt while autographing a giant boxing glove signed by more than 100 boxing champions.

James Corbett vs. John L. Sullivan

In 1892 you could buy a loaf of bread for a nickel. But a ticket to the James Corbett/John L. Sullivan fight would set you back as much as $15.

In 1892 you could buy a comfortable house for about $2,000. But the Corbett/Sullivan purse was a whopping $25,000. It was a big fight.

There were lots of reasons. For one, it was long overdue and highly anticipated. Sullivan had first claimed the heavyweight title in 1885, but from 1889 to 1892 didn't defend it, participating only in exhibitions while concurrently pursuing an acting career. Corbett, meanwhile, had battled some of the top heavyweights of the era while waiting for a shot at the champ.

▲ This is an actual ticket from the 1892 Corbett/Sullivan fight.

For another, the fight matched two men in stark contrast to one another. Sullivan was a bare-knuckle brawler, a gregarious personality who was most at home in a tavern when he wasn't in the ring; Corbett was a bank teller who primarily fought under the Marquess of Queensbury rules and earned the nickname "Gentleman Jim."

In fact, the fight would be the first for the heavyweight title that was conducted under the Queensbury rules: padded gloves, three-minute rounds, and one minute between each round.

So on September 7, 1892, some 10,000 fans packed the the Olympic Club in New Orleans to watch Corbett and Sullivan cap three days of boxing that was billed as the "Carnival of Champions."

▲ Sullivan wore these gloves in an exhibition fight prior to the big match with Corbett.

Sullivan was a heavy favorite who outweighed his opponent by 25 pounds. And indeed, the fight turned out to be a mismatch. But it was Corbett who won easily.

At 26, the challenger was seven years younger than the champion, and he nimbly countered Sullivan's attacks by keeping mobile in the ring and picking his spots. In the third round, Corbett broke Sullivan's nose with a left.

As the fight wore on, Sullivan could offer less and less resistance, and in the 21st round, Corbett landed a combination that sent the champion to the ground. The fight was over, and boxing had a new heavyweight champ.

▲ After the big fight, this special "Registered Hits" booklet let fans who weren't there in person relive the entire fight, almost blow-by-blow.

▼ Corbett wore these actual gloves while defeating Sullivan in 1892 in the first championship boxing match in which gloves were used.

▲ This bronze of Sullivan shows him striking a classic bare-knuckle brawler's pose.

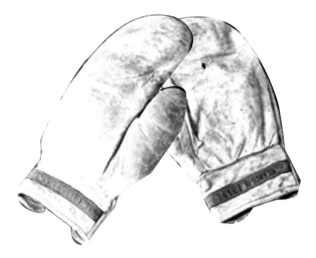

James Jeffries vs. Jack Johnson

▲ Here is an actual ticket to one of the most heralded fights of the century. The ticket is autographed by famed fight promoter Tex Rickard on the back.

In the end, James Jeffries left the ring stunned, staggered, bleeding, and walking with the help of his seconds and friends.

Jack Johnson left the ring standing, unfazed and unhurt.

The much-heralded heavyweight championship match of 1910 turned out to be no match at all.

Five years after retiring as the heavyweight champion, undefeated in 22 career fights, Jeffries was persuaded to leave his post-boxing career as an alfalfa farmer and return to the ring to fight Johnson, a man three years younger and in the prime of his career.

He was persuaded because Johnson was black and Jeffries was not. Jeffries was the "Great White Hope."

After Jeffries retired in 1905, he was succeeded by champions Marvin Hart and Tommy Burns. In 1908, Johnson, the son of an American slave, knocked out Burns in Sydney, Australia, to become the first black man to win the heavyweight title.

That didn't sit well with much of an America that was less than 50 years removed from the end of the Civil War.

▲ Style of the times: Jeffries wore this fighting shirt and ring shoes. The belt, honoring his Irish heritage, was one of many he was given for his pugilistic skills.

> Patterson, N.J.
>
> Dear Robert;
> I received your very nice letter, with the pictures enclosed, for which I thank you very much. It was nice and thoughtful of you to send them to me. You are one of the first newspapermen who has ever kept his word about sending pictures.
> In return for your kindness I am going to accept your invitation to come out to the boxing classes at Princeton; if you will please let me know by mail which day you select for me to come. You could tell the boys I'll be there on the appointed day, and I'll be very glad to come over there.
> Thank you for your letter. I hope you are in the best of health and enjoying life to the full. Best regards to you,
>
> Yours sincerely,
> Jack Johnson
>
> 6/13/1936.

▲ Jack Johnson signed this 1936 letter to a sportswriter thanking him for sending photos. In appreciation, Johnson indicates that he will accept the writer's invitation to attend boxing classes at Princeton.

The Incomparable
PRIZE FIGHT
AT
Reno - July 4, 1910

JACK JOHNSON vs JIM JEFFRIES
HEAVYWEIGHT
BATTLE OF CHAMPIONS

▲ This fight poster was part of the national publicity campaign for the fight that drew 30,000 fans to Reno.

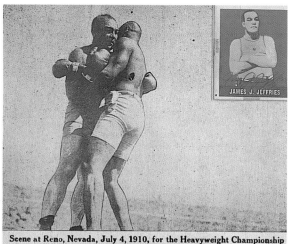

Scene at Reno, Nevada, July 4, 1910, for the Heavyweight Championship of the World.
JAMES J. JEFFRIES vs. JACK JOHNSON.
Won by Johnson 15th round, knockout.

▲ This photo card shows action from the Jeffries/Johnson bout. The color card in the top corner is autographed by Jeffries.

Johnson's outspoken personality, and his marriage to a white woman, only fueled the bigotry.

On July 4, 1910, the two boxers met before more than 30,000 fans in Reno, Nevada. Johnson was cautious and defensive at the fight's outset, but it quickly became apparent that Jeffries, though fighting with heart, was no match for the current champion.

Johnson soon began to wear him down. By the seventh round, Jeffries' right eye was nearly swollen shut. In the 14th round, he was knocked to the mat for the first time in his career. And in the 15th round, when Johnson's blows sent Jeffries reeling, the former champion's corner threw in the towel.

Johnson had retained his title. He would remain the heavyweight champ until 1915, when he was knocked out by Jess Willard in a controversial battle. Johnson later claimed he threw the fight; see his letter about the bout on page 165.

▲ Jack Johnson's fighting trunks were typical of the day, with a wide, elastic belt and tight, knee-length leggings.

▲ Tools of the trade: Jeffries wore the gloves at top in the early 1900s; Johnson wore the bottom set later in his career.

Jack Dempsey vs. Gene Tunney

▼ Gene Tunney used these gloves (top) in his famous "Long Count" fight against Jack Dempsey in 1927. Dempsey used the gloves at bottom in a fight against Georges Carpentier.

▲ Tunney and Dempsey were no strangers when they fought in 1927. This program is from their earlier fight in 1926 in Philadelphia.

It was September 22, 1927. Heavyweight boxing champion Gene Tunney lay sprawled on the mat midway through round seven, challenger Jack Dempsey standing over him, 104,000 fans at Chicago's Soldier Field screaming wildly.

One . . .

Dempsey, a former champ who had 50 knockouts in his career, could hardly wait for Tunney to stand up so he could deliver another blow.

Two . . .

Trouble was, Dempsey was required by rule to go to the furthest neutral corner, and referee Dave Barry motioned him away.

Three . . .

Tunney hadn't moved, but neither had Dempsey, so Barry pushed him toward the far corner.

Four . . .

Dempsey finally got the message and retreated.

Five . . .

Now Barry turned his attention to the fallen Tunney. But instead of picking up his count at six, with the timekeeper, the referee began at the start. One . . .

At nine, Tunney got to his feet. He had been down 14 seconds. But he was not out. The champion, who had controlled most of the match to that point, regained his poise and finished out the last two rounds. He defeated Dempsey by unanimous decision.

In fairness to Tunney, he had raised his head at the count of three and insisted he could have gotten up but saw the referee's count. Still, the Long

▲ This ticket would have gotten you into one of the most famous and controversial bouts in boxing history, and it would have cost you $40.

▼ Dempsey signed these trunks that he wore during the famous "Long Count" bout against Gene Tunney in 1927.

Count would go down in boxing lore.

Tunney would fight just once more, defeating Tom Heeney in 1928, before retiring as champion with a career record of 65–2–1.

Dempsey retired after the fight, concluding a 64–6–9 career. Two of the defeats were to Tunney, with the Long Count fight actually a rematch of their bout 364 days earlier at Sesquicentennial Stadium in Philadelphia.

Some 120,000 fans had witnessed that earlier fight. Dempsey was throttled, losing his heavyweight crown, but provided one of sports' all-time famous quotes afterward.

When his wife, actress Estelle Taylor, asked him what happened, Dempsey told her, "Honey, I forgot to duck."

Immortal Encounter

My pursuit of Jack Dempsey mementos was frustrating and prolonged. I first learned that Dempsey's memorabilia was stored in a military academy in Hesperia, California. The academy headmaster, a Mr. Rhoades, assured me that he would hand over the items if I could obtain authorization from Dempsey. I did just that, and quickly contacted the headmaster, but 12 months and 20 calls later, I still had not received anything.

I called him one final time. He told me that Jack Dempsey's daughter, Joan, had picked up all of her father's items. But Joan told me that the items never were given to her, but to a curator from a historical museum in San Bernardino, California. I was livid.

At the museum's invitation, my wife and I traveled to California and browsed through Dempsey's items in awe. The curator asked me if I saw anything of interest. "Yes," I said. "All of it."

But I could have none of it. Told that I would have to submit a list of items for approval, I was furious. I had come all the way to California only to be frustrated again. I called Joan Dempsey, who invited Marcia and I to her house in Los Angeles.

Joan, it turned out, was also concerned about the fate of her father's mementos and agreed to help me recover them. She presented me with a few of the rare items that remained in her possession. Joan was a wonderful person. If not for her, my second trip out west would have been a total loss.

Finally, weeks later, I received a box from the museum, filled with treasure. Among the items were the gloves Dempsey used when he defeated Georges Carpentier in 1921, Dempsey's shoes from the legendary brawl with Luis Angel Firpo, and more than 100 framed photos.

In 1993 I added Dempsey's heavyweight title belt and a wall-size oil painting of his fight with Jess Willard in 1919.

—JOEL PLATT

Joe Louis vs. Billy Conn

Twelve rounds into their scheduled fifteen-round bout at the Polo Grounds on June 18, 1941, 174-pound Billy Conn had the upper hand against 200-pound Joe Louis, beating the heavyweight champion on two of the three judges' scorecards (the third called it a draw).

Conn was a former light-heavyweight champion who had proven he could box with just about anyone. After winning the vacant title in 1939 by beating Melio Bettina, Conn beat future heavyweight title challenger Gus Dorazio. Later, he retained his crown in a rematch with Bettina, and defended it with a victory over future champ Gus Lesnevich.

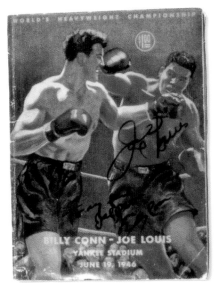

▼ Both Louis and Conn autographed this program from the 1946 rematch of their epic 1941 bout.

But the "Brown Bomber" clearly was out of Conn's class—or so most people thought. Louis had won the heavyweight title with an eighth-round knockout of James J. Braddock in Chicago in 1937. He went on to defeat all of the top heavy-weight challengers, including a first-round knockout at Yankee Stadium of Germany's Max Schmeling, who had handed Louis his first defeat in 1936.

Louis, whose popularity transcended color lines, would forge one of the most remarkable careers in boxing history, winning 68 of 71 matches, 54 by knockout. But he

▲ Louis wore these gloves when he knocked out Billy Conn in 1946. Conn and Louis signed a photo of the fight (left). Also pictured are a fight ticket and an advertisement signed by Conn.

▼ The crown on the back of Joe Louis' heavy wool robe is embroidered with the names of fighters that Louis defeated during his great career in the ring.

▲ This leather championship belt commemorates Louis' long reign as heavyweight champion.

was on the ropes against Conn, whose speed and quickness were neutralizing Louis' strength.

"You've got to knock him out," Louis' handlers told him.

Over in the other corner, Conn's men, aware that he was winning, told him to be cautious.

Louis listened; Conn did not.

Conn made the ill-fated decision to press his advantage and go for a knockout—just the kind of fight he knew going in that he wouldn't win. Given a reprieve, Louis slugged it out with Conn in the 13th round and knocked him out with two seconds left.

Still, in defeat Conn had gained a large measure of respect. After Louis served in the army and Conn in the navy during World War II, the two fought one more time. That time, Louis knocked out Conn in the eighth round.

Immortal Encounter

I became friends with Billy Conn's sons, Tom and Billy Jr., while I was a student at Duquesne University. They often invited me to visit their home in Squirrel Hill, near Pittsburgh, so I could talk to their father about his career.

I asked Billy, who was known as the "Pittsburgh Kid," why he abandoned his boxing strategy against Louis in their bout in 1941. Conn, ahead on the judges' cards through 12 rounds, apparently needed only to fight the champ even over the final 3 rounds to secure a stunning upset. But the underdog went for the knockout; instead, he was knocked out by Louis in the 13th round.

Here's what Conn said: "I never told anyone this before, but I knew I couldn't beat Joe Louis in New York if the fight went the distance. The mob was behind Joe and controlled the fights. Unless I knocked him out, there was no way I would ever get the decision.

Everyone said I had won 10 of the first 12 rounds, but when we went to check with the judges, the scorecards disappeared and didn't turn up until two days after the fight."

In 1979 I visited Joe Louis at the Holiday House Hotel in Pittsburgh. I had already obtained Louis' commemorative belt, gloves, robes, and trunks from his family. When I asked the champ if he would sign the items, he kindly obliged and told me that he was pleased to know that his things were part of the Sports Immortals collection.

Joe told me that he and Conn remained close friends even after their second meeting in 1946, when he knocked out his foe in the eighth round.

I asked Joe about their first fight.

"I guess I just got lucky in the 13th round," he said. "The Pittsburgh Kid gave me one of my toughest fights ever!"

—**JOEL PLATT**

Ray Robinson vs. Jake LaMotta

▲ Jake LaMotta autographed this championship fight program from a bout against Sugar Ray Robinson.

On February 14, 1951, boxing legend Sugar Ray Robinson stepped into the ring against middleweight champion Jake LaMotta, the "Bronx Bull."

This was not unusual. In fact, it was the sixth time since 1942 that the longtime rivals had met. But it was noteworthy because it would be the last time. And it would be the most memorable of all their bouts.

Sugar Ray, then a welterweight, hadn't lost a bout in his career until LaMotta, a middleweight, stopped his winning streak at 40 fights with a 10-round decision in Detroit in 1943.

LaMotta had been among Robinson's first 40 victims in New York a year earlier. But the fight was brutally tough, with Sugar Ray winning by decision after 10 rounds. In Detroit, the judges' cards went to LaMotta—Robinson's first career loss and his only loss for the next eight years. Robinson would avenge that defeat three weeks later in Detroit and twice more in 1945. If there was any payback left, it came in their final meeting in 1951.

LaMotta first won the middleweight crown in 1949 by knocking out champion Marcel Cerdan. A year later he successfully defended the title

Immortal Encounter

Sugar Ray often is considered, pound for pound, the greatest fighter of all time. His last fight took place in Pittsburgh against Joey Archer at the Civic Arena.

One day before that fight, a good friend of the champ, Woogie Harris, introduced him to me. I told Sugar Ray about the Sports Immortals Museum and that I would appreciate any memento that he could donate to the collection.

The champ was very impressed and told me to come by his dressing room after the fight—he would be happy to give me his gloves and trunks. Unfortunately, Sugar Ray was at the nadir of his career and received

a terrible beating from Archer that night. He was so bloody after the fight that he was convinced that it was time to hang up the gloves.

When I entered the dressing room after the fight, I found myself staring at a wounded warrior. Sugar Ray was sitting on a bench, still bleeding from the facial wounds he suffered in the ring. It was sad to see this great champion in such a horrid state. Looking up from the floor, he said to me, "Joel, if you still want my gloves and trunks with all this blood on them, they're yours."

—JOEL PLATT

against Tiberio Mitri and Laurent Dauthuille, knocking out the latter in the 15th round while trailing on the judges' cards.

Meanwhile, Robinson had captured the vacant welterweight title with a victory over Tommy Bell in 1946. He successfully defended that crown numerous times before his last fight with LaMotta.

The early rounds of the fight at Chicago Stadium gave little indication of what was to come, with LaMotta hanging close. But Robinson's overpowering strength and athleticism were too much, and he gradually wore down his foe.

By the late rounds, LaMotta was absorbing terrible punishment. The fight was stopped in the 13th round, and Robinson had earned the crown. His victory was so overwhelming that it came to be known as the "St. Valentine's Day Massacre."

▲ Robinson presented the gloves and trunks he wore in his last fight against Joey Archer in 1965 to Joel Platt.

▲ Robinson was awarded this championship belt on March 25, 1958, after defeating Carmen Basilio to win the middleweight title for the fifth time.

Muhammad Ali vs. Sonny Liston

▲ This special press pass allowed access to the 1964 Clay/Liston bout, whose result ended up stunning the boxing world.

▼ One of Sports Immortals' most memorable acquisitions came when Joel Platt received these sweat pants from the champ himself. Ali had worn them while training to fight Sonny Liston and Floyd Patterson.

When heavyweight champion Sonny Liston stayed on the stool in his corner and didn't come out for the seventh round against challenger Cassius Clay in Miami Beach in 1964, fight fans howled. How could the man who was one of the most intimidating and courageous fighters ever to step into the ring throw in the towel against such a huge underdog?

That question and others would hound Liston all his life.

Liston had a huge reach, a large fist, and one of the most powerful jabs in boxing history. He originally won the heavyweight title when he knocked out Floyd Patterson in the first round in a bout in 1962.

That was no fluke. When the two met in a rematch a year later, Liston knocked him out in the first round again.

Liston would go on to amass 50 victories—39 by knockout, including 8 in the first round—in 54 fights. But he did not limit his altercations to the ring, and he was arrested numerous times, including once for assaulting a police officer.

Liston blamed the debacle in Miami Beach on a shoulder injury and, a year later, a rematch was held in Lewiston, Maine, in front of only 2,434 fans.

But instead of answering questions, the rematch merely created more when Liston went down in the first round. The bout would forever be shrouded in mystery, with the knockout known as Ali's "Phantom Punch." Did he or didn't he land a crushing blow?

The question never was clearly answered. Liston's life ended as troubled as he lived it. In December 1970 he was found dead in his Las Vegas apartment, apparently from a drug overdose.

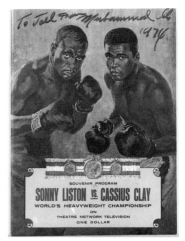

▲ Ali (then Cassius Clay) took another giant leap on the way to superstardom with the victory over Liston. This autographed program is from that 1964 fight.

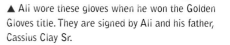

▲ Ali wore these gloves when he won the Golden Gloves title. They are signed by Ali and his father, Cassius Clay Sr.

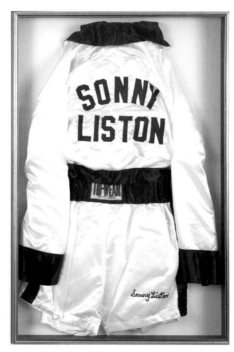

▲ Sonny Liston wore this robe and trunks during his career.

◄ One of Ali's championship belts.

Ali, meanwhile, became the single most important figure in boxing history, and perhaps in all of sports. His popularity was matched by only a handful of people in any field. He remains one of the world's most recognizable and beloved people.

No one who saw it will ever forget Ali's emotional appearance at the torch-lighting ceremony at the 1996 Summer Olympics in Atlanta. When the champ held aloft the torch, his arm shaking slightly, it instantly became one of the most memorable moments in sports. A lifetime of living only one way—his own—had finally earned Ali the world's unfettered acclaim.

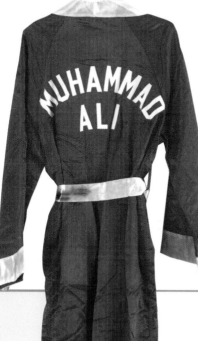

▲ Ali himself wore this robe while creating visuals for a computerized fight against Rocky Marciano.

Immortal Encounter

In traveling a million miles for a million mementos, the one Immortal who stands out as the greatest is without a doubt Muhammad Ali. I met Ali four times, and each encounter was unique, with its own special meaning.

I first met the champ in 1964, shortly after his first victory over Sonny Liston. Ali was training at Miami's 5th Street Gym for the Liston rematch. I had met trainer Angelo Dundee at another fight and told him about Sports Immortals. After Ali's workout, Dundee introduced us and I gave him information on the collection. Ali grabbed the brochure and motioned me to follow him upstairs.

In his dressing room, I said, "Champ, my father has been an avid boxing fan all his life. He thinks you and Jack Johnson are the greatest heavyweights of all time." Ali smiled and began to dance around and throw lightning quick jabs in the air. Then he said, "Joel, your dad is right! I am a big Sugar Ray Robinson. I am the greatest!" Ali then had his favorite corner man, Bundini Brown, get the athletic suit that Ali wore while training for the Liston fight. The champ presented me with the suit and autographed it to the museum. For the first time in my life I was at a loss for words. I thanked Ali and confirmed that he was indeed the greatest of all time.

In 1977 I met him again at his training facility in Deer Lake, Pennsylvania. I reminded him of our first meeting in Miami, and mentioned that we were commissioning a life-size wax figure of him for the museum. I asked him for trunks, gloves, and a robe to put on the statue. Once again,

he came through, calling for his valet and telling him, "Get my friend Joel Platt everything he needs!" The valet told Ali he had only one robe left, the one he wore in his last fight. "Get the robe!" Ali shouted. "The man only asked for one robe!"

Three years later, I was back at Deer Lake, not knowing at the time it would be Ali's last camp. I had brought programs from his greatest fights for him to sign. While I waited, he sparred first with Eddie Mustafa Muhammad and then with singer Tom Jones, who was also visiting the camp. Though Ali was delayed several times, he postponed his dinner to make sure he could sign all the programs.

"You tell them I'll be there in 20 minutes," he said. "My friend Joel has been waiting here all day for me to sign his items, and I am not going to let him down."

He didn't let me down and I remain forever grateful.

In 1987 I was able to obtain Ali's championship belt and the robe he wore in 1960 at the Olympic Games in Rome. Several years later, I went with my son Jim to see Ali in Philadelphia. As we walked into the hotel room, filled with people visiting the champ, Ali called out, "It's my man, the museum man!"

"It was a moment I'll never forget," Jim said. "After all these years, Ali never forgot my father."

Thanks, Champ, I'll never forget you, either.

—JOEL PLATT

Ray Leonard vs. Marvin Hagler

Former lightweight and welter-weight champion Sugar Ray Leonard was ringside in 1986 when middleweight champion "Marvelous" Marvin Hagler successfully defended his title against John the "Beast" Mugabi.

Leonard turned to the friend sitting next to him, actor Michael J. Fox. "I can beat this guy," Sugar Ray said. "I can beat this guy."

And so, three years removed from his last fight, a knockout of Kevin Howard, Leonard went back to the future. He would come out of retirement for the second time to face Hagler in Las Vegas for the WBC middleweight title.

Hagler first ascended to the middleweight throne by knocking out champion Alan Minter in 1980. He successfully defended his title 12 times (only two bouts shy of the all-time record) over the next six years before agreeing to take on Leonard.

▲ Here is one of Sugar Ray's boxing robes, along with an autographed photo of the talented champion.

Sugar Ray, perhaps boxing's most charismatic personality since Muhammad Ali, had originally retired from competition in 1982 after suffering a detached retina in his eye. He came out of retirement to fight Howard, but left the sport again.

▲ From the SuperFight in 1987 at Caesars Palace in Las Vegas: an original fight program, a ticket to the bout, and training gloves signed by both fighters.

Leonard was seeking to win the title in three different weight classes, but few experts gave him a chance against the bigger, stronger, and younger (by two years) Hagler.

But Sugar Ray trained every day for a year, bringing in volunteers to step into the ring with him as tune-ups—and to get used to being hit again. Most importantly, Leonard hadn't lost any of his hand speed, which was evident from the beginning of the fight with the reigning champ. As the rounds went on, Sugar Ray defied the critics simply by standing in against Hagler.

When the 12 rounds were over, it was too close for the ringside spectators to call. In a split decision, the judges' cards went to Sugar Ray. It was one of the greatest upsets in boxing history.

Football

▲ Clockwise from top left: Ken Strong kicking shoe; Deacon Jones' last jersey with the Redskins; football statue c. 1900; John Elway game jersey; Merlin Olsen helmet; Emmitt Smith game jersey; Red Grange-autographed 1925 Illinois program; 1972 Dolphins autographed program; football used in 1921 Notre Dame/Michigan game; 1914 Harvard/Yale program; football signed by Ernie Nevers, Red Grange, and Bronko Nagurski; Byron "Whizzer" White game jersey; autographed Knute Rockne photograph.

Immortals Who Inspire

Here are stories of athletes whose achievement of character exceeded their achievements of skill.

George Gipp & Knute Rockne

Athletes have looked to other athletes for inspiration since the first Greeks ran races in the ancient Olympics. In modern times, the most famous athletic inspiration comes from college football.

George Gipp was an outstanding athlete in high school, but he never played football. At Notre Dame, legendary coach Knute Rockne recognized the speedy and athletic Gipp as a future star, and he was right. In four years with the Fighting Irish, Gipp scored 21 touchdowns as a halfback, and was the nation's top defensive back as well. He became the first of many Notre Dame players to be named All-America performers, and helped Rockne build the program that would become college football's most successful.

Late in Gipp's senior season, he got a throat infection that quickly worsened. Medicine had no answer, and Gipp faded quickly. Rockne visited the gallant young man in the hospital and, as the story goes, Gipp told Rockne to remember him and his struggle. "Someday, when the breaks are beating the boys, tell them to win one for the Gipper."

Eight years later, Rockne did just that, using Gipp's inspiration to rally a Notre Dame team to a thrilling comeback win over mighty Army. The phrase "win one for the Gipper" entered the language and has been used in sports and many other walks of life. Gipp's courage in the face of death and his dying thoughts for his teammates are examples that anyone, whether in sports or out, can look to for inspiration.

Jerry Kramer

When he was a college football star at Fordham, Vince Lombardi was a lineman, one of the famous "Seven Blocks of Granite."

When he took over the Green Bay Packers as their head coach in 1959, he knew that he would need an equally hard guy to anchor the offensive line. Lombardi found his man in guard Jerry Kramer. The Montana native had joined the Packers out of the University of Idaho in 1958; he would be a key component of Green Bay's championship teams for the next decade.

Behind Kramer, backs like Paul Hornung and Jim Taylor ran for touchdowns and thousands of yards. Quarterback Bart Starr knew that he was safe from assaulting linemen thanks to Kramer and his linemates. Kramer and tackle Fuzzy Thurston formed perhaps the most devastating sweep block tandem in NFL history.

▲ Actor and future president Ronald Reagan wore this helmet when he portrayed Notre Dame hero George Gipp (autographed photo, top) in the movie *Knute Rockne: All-American*. Reagan wrote to Sports Immortals about it (letter, bottom).

Kramer's most memorable play came in the bone-chilling 1967 NFL Championship Game, the fabled "Ice Bowl." Unbowed by wind-chill conditions that dipped to 30 below, Kramer led Bart Starr over the goal line from the 1-yard line in the final minute to clinch the fourth of Green Bay's five NFL championships in the decade.

But why was Kramer so inspirational? Simple. He kept showing up and performing at a consistently high level even though he underwent 22 operations to keep his battered body on the field. He has so many surgical scars that he was known as "Zipper." In an age before physical therapy and high-tech diagnostic tools or even arthroscopic surgery, Kramer climbed out of the hospital time and again to face the best the NFL had to offer, and to win.

Tom Dempsey

Football players spend a lot of time overcoming injuries and pain. They battle against the little bruises of daily play and rehab from injuries that knock them out of the lineup. They usually recover. They have all their parts and they strap on the helmet, whole again.

Tom Dempsey didn't have that luxury. His disabilities were permanent, part of his life from birth. But also part of his life from birth was a burning desire to not let his physical problems stop him from living the life he wanted, and from playing the sport he loved.

Dempsey was born with a right arm that ended just below the elbow and a right clubfoot. He had trouble walking, let alone running, but he didn't let that get in his way, competing as a lineman in junior and high school football. He actually found that his partial foot was a positive in the kicking game. Using a special shoe with a flat front, he used a straight-ahead kicking style and the bulk of his 255 pounds to smack field goals. Amazingly, Dempsey persevered and signed with the New Orleans Saints in 1969; he went on to play for five teams in 11 NFL seasons.

In his second year with New Orleans he became more than just a player who exceeded his physical limitations; he became a legend. On November 8, 1970, he lined up at his own 37-yard line for a field goal that, if successful, would win the game over the Lions. The snap was good, the spot was down, and Dempsey slugged the ball. It dropped over the crossbar 63 yards away, setting an all-time NFL record.

Half a foot was better than one, better than all the other feet that ever kicked the ball. Though Denver's Jason Elam tied the mark in 1998, no one has topped it, and few players ever have topped Dempsey's determination to overcome obstacles.

▲ Jerry Kramer wore this uniform as one of the bedrock members of the five-time NFL champion Green Bay Packers.

▼ Sports Immortals is proud to display this unique kicking shoe made specially for Tom Dempsey. It is the same model he wore when he kicked an NFL-record 63-yard field goal in 1970.

Jim Thorpe

▲ In 1952, Thorpe autographed this rare football photo of himself, taken during his days at Carlisle.

From a hardscrabble home on a dusty reservation in Oklahoma, Jim Thorpe fashioned the greatest all-around sports career of all time. And though he is perhaps best known for his stunning accomplishments in the Olympics (see pages 116-117), Thorpe first made his mark on the football field.

The story goes that he was walking by the track at the Carlisle Indian School in Pennsylvania one day when he saw some students doing the high jump. Wearing overalls, Thorpe supposedly outjumped them all, having never tried the event. Soon he was starring for the track team and his speed was being put to use on the football squad.

Carlisle, helped by Thorpe and led by legendary coach Pop Warner, put together a powerful team, but few of the established schools were willing to play the tiny institution. That fact—and football history—would change in 1911 when powerful Harvard played host to Carlisle.

The matchup didn't seem fair. Harvard hadn't lost at all in 1910, and would not lose in 1912, 1913, or 1914 either. But in a stunning upset, Thorpe led Carlisle with hard-hitting defense, dominating running, and unerring kicking. In one of college football's most surprising upsets, Carlisle won 18–15, and Thorpe became a star.

After the season, Thorpe became the first Native American named All-America; he was named again in 1912 after scoring 25 touchdowns and helping Carlisle become one of the smallest schools ever to win the national championship.

Thorpe's final college football season was 1912, but that wasn't the end of his football career. In 1915 he joined a pro team, the Canton Bulldogs, and helped them win three championships. In 1920 he was named president of a new pro league that would become, in 1922, today's National Football League (NFL). Thorpe played until 1926, including a season with the short-lived Oorang Indians, a team he formed using all Native-American players. In 1963 he was named a charter member of the Pro Football Hall of Fame.

▲ Along with football gear Thorpe himself used at Carlisle are mementos of his other exploits: an autographed baseball, a program from the 1912 Olympics, and a program from the Canton Bulldogs. The beaded gloves were handmade by Thorpe while a Carlisle student.

Red Grange

▲ This one-of-a-kind Red Grange doll was part of a special set created for the 1933 World's Fair in Chicago.

▲ This is a rare Wilson Sporting Goods advertising display from the 1920s, featuring Red Grange promoting a Knute Rockne model football.

Few players can be said to have revolutionized a sport; fewer still can claim that responsibility twice over. One such player was Harold "Red" Grange, who first helped propel college football to previously unreached popularity and later made pro football a legitimate national sport.

Grange combined sprinter's speed with unmatched moves and fierce determination. As a high school runner, he scored 75 touchdowns in three seasons. In his first college season in 1923, he scored 12 touchdowns and helped Illinois win the national title.

In 1924 he became a legend. On October 18, 1924, Grange took apart a mighty Michigan team, ending the Wolverines' 20-game winning streak and earning his famous nickname—the Galloping Ghost.

He took the opening kickoff and returned it 95 yards for a touchdown. In the next 12 minutes, he scored three more times on field-spanning, tackler-dodging runs of 67, 56, and 44 yards. In the previous two seasons, Michigan had allowed four touchdowns; Grange had matched that total in less than a quarter.

He scored later on an 11-yard run and then threw a 20-yard touchdown pass. In the Illini's 39–14 win, Grange piled up a stunning 402 total yards passing, running, and returning kicks.

After the game, famed sportswriter Grantland Rice wrote a poem that contained the lines ". . . a gray ghost thrown into the game/that rival hands may never touch," and from then on, the Galloping Ghost ran atop the football world.

▲ Grange autographed this photo of himself in his famous No. 77 jersey to his friend, Sports Immortals founder Joel Platt.

Grange turned pro in 1925. At the time, the NFL played second-fiddle to the college game, but Grange's entry instantly bumped the pro league up in class. A barnstorming tour by Grange's Chicago Bears attracted hundreds of thousands; the NFL had its first star.

A knee injury in 1927 ended Grange's days of greatness, though he played effectively until 1934. His time on stage was relatively brief, but Grange created a ground-breaking record of achievement on the gridiron.

▲ Grange signed and donated this unique jersey from a special All-Star game to the Sports Immortals Museum.

Immortal Encounter

As I approached the door of Red Grange's home in Indian Lake Estates, Florida, in 1976, I noticed two live alligators sleeping on the grass in front of the house. Red's wife, Muggs, sensed my apprehension and told me not to worry. "They won't bother you if you don't bother them," she said. She led me into the living room and called Red in from the backyard.

We sat down, and I interviewed Red about his playing days. We spoke for three hours reminiscing about his college career at Illinois and how he revolutionized professional football when he signed a contract with George Halas to play for the Chicago Bears. I asked Red to compare the players of his time with those who are playing today. He said, "Greatness transcends time. The players who were great in my day would be stars today."

In Red's opinion, Bronko Nagurski was the greatest player who ever lived. When I asked who had the greatest impact on his life Red quickly replied, "Father Flanagan of Boys' Town was the greatest person I ever met, and Ty Cobb was the athlete I most admired."

I showed the Granges my museum brochure and told them about my goal to perpetuate the memories of sports immortals. Red signed an All-Star football jersey and presented me with an autographed football,

Chicago Bears championship game programs, and autographed photos.

Red and Muggs Grange were two of the nicest people I have met and I visited with them on several occasions. I found Red to be a very humble individual who never let his fame affect his personality.

My final encounter with Red came in 1990. I commissioned the famous sports artist Robert Stephen Simon to create a large oil painting depicting the Chicago Bears' owner and coach George Halas surrounded by the four great running backs in Bears history: Walter Payton, Gale Sayers, Bronko Nagurski, and Grange. [See page 110.]

The painting was forwarded to Red for his signature. After staring at the painting for more than 15 minutes, Red became teary eyed. He cleared his throat and said, "This is the greatest painting I ever saw. I am honored to be included."

Several weeks later, I received a thank you note from Red saying, "Joel, your collection is a tribute to your love and dedication to sports. Good luck, your pal Red." Red passed away several months later in 1991. It was an honor and privilege to call the "Galloping Ghost" a special friend. **—JOEL PLATT**

Sid Luckman

▲ Trophy presented to Sid Luckman in honor of his many NFL accomplishments.

Throughout the NFL's first decade, the pathway to victory was on the ground. Passing was rare and even more rarely successful, and the aerial circus that is the NFL today was years away.

The Orville and Wilbur Wright of the NFL was Chicago quarterback Sid Luckman, the player most responsible for making passing a big part of NFL offenses. It was his success with the new T formation in the 1940s that opened coaches and fans' eyes to the potential of the pass.

Luckman came to the NFL after being a great single-wing quarterback at Columbia University, but he was switched to the then-newfangled T formation in the pros. In 1940 he was the man at the controls when the Bears beat the Washington Redskins 73–0 in the NFL title game, still the league's single-game record for points scored. And from then on, it was off to the skyway as Luckman's adept passing and quick feet helped him set new standards.

His greatest passing game occurred in 1943, when he was on his way to setting new NFL records for passing yards, touchdown passes, and being

Immortal Encounter

In 1965 I entered the lobby of Sid Luckman's lush Chicago lakefront apartment building. I didn't know Sid's apartment number, but I asked the doorman if the former Bears quarterback was in town.

The attendant said no, and began to call their apartment to convince me. Just then, Sid and his wife pulled up in a taxi, having just returned from a long vacation. I introduced myself and told him about my collection. Sid was interested and invited me upstairs.

I took in their incredible view of Lake Michigan, and once Sid settled in, I told him about my vision for the Sports Immortals Museum.

"Joel, that's a great idea," Sid said. "I'll be glad to help in any way possible." He searched his apartment for a jersey, but was unable to locate one. Instead, Sid brought out a trophy and an autographed program from a game against the Washington Redskins in which he threw five touchdown passes. I

told Sid how much I appreciated his kindness and promised to keep in touch.

Over the years, Sid and I became good friends, and I would often visit him after he moved to Aventura, Florida. The day I found out that Sid had passed away was very sad for me. Sid was a great athlete and a special person. In all my travels, he was the nicest human being I have ever met.

Shortly after Sid's death, his daughter, Ellen, contacted me to let me know that her father wanted me to have some of his most prized possessions for the Sports Immortals Museum. These included an original letter written by George Halas to Sid as the legendary "Papa Bear" was dying, as well as the football that Sid presented to his mother after throwing an NFL-record seven touchdown passes against the New York Giants on November 14, 1943.

—JOEL PLATT

▲ On the left is a letter written by Luckman, describing his greatest game, the 1943 NFL Championship Game. On the right is an autographed program from that contest, in which the Bears defeated the Redskins 41–21 and Luckman threw five touchdown passes.

named the league MVP. On November 14, 1943, the Bears visited the New York Giants at the Polo Grounds. The Giants and their fans honored their opponent—and hometown Manhattan boy—by holding Sid Luckman Day. Sid made the most of his day by becoming the first player to throw seven touchdown passes in one game, a feat matched only four times since. The Bears won the game 56–7, and Luckman signed over the game ball from his special day to his mother.

He gave her another present at the end of the season, when he again led the Bears to a title-game romp over the Redskins, 41–21, a game in which Luckman had five touchdown passes.

Luckman continued to refine his passing skills, and by the time he retired in 1950, his success had firmly established passing as a key weapon in football.

▲ This is a letter from George Halas to Luckman, in which Halas writes, "My boy, my pride in you has no bounds. You were the consummate player. I love you with all my heart."

▲ When Luckman passed away in 1998, his daughter, Ellen, presented this ball to the Sports Immortals Museum, calling it "one of my father's most prized possessions. He wanted Joel Platt to receive it."

The 1958 NFL Championship Game

▲ Johnny Unitas wore this helmet for the Baltimore Colts while virtually inventing the now-standard "two-minute drill."

Once in a great while, a game is played that changes the sport. That is, a single sporting event is so influential, so striking, so era-making, that it stands apart from other games, becoming the sort of thing writer Robert Hughes calls a "hinge in history."

Such an event was the 1958 NFL Championship Game between the Baltimore Colts and the New York Giants.

By the middle part of the 1950s, the pro game had come a long way from its second-fiddle roots, but it still paled in comparison to the national popularity of college football. In 1951 the league's title game was first broadcast on television, setting the stage for the NFL's great leap forward. By 1958 television ownership had risen dramatically and viewership was up. Also, fans and networks alike were beginning to appreciate the natural marriage between television and a sport played in a steady stream of stop-and-start moments on a rectangular field.

It all came together on December 28, 1958, when the Baltimore Colts, led by quarterback Johnny Unitas, traveled to Yankee Stadium to take on the New York Giants for the NFL title. TV viewers got a very special treat, as the two teams put on a fantastic show of back-and-forth action, with great plays, game-turning moments, and a cast of characters that included no less than 12 future Hall of Famers.

But it was the show's finale that really captured the public's attention and suddenly made the NFL the darling of the sports world.

Trailing 17–14 late in the game, Unitas led one of his patented two-minute drills, taking Baltimore 86 yards in

▼ Game-used jerseys from two of the stars of the 1958 NFL title game: defensive end Geno Marchetti (No. 89) and wide reciever Raymond Berry (No. 82), both members of the Pro Football Hall of Fame.

1:56. Baltimore's Steve Myrha kicked a field goal with seven seconds left to tie the game. For the first time ever, the NFL Championship Game would go to overtime, while millions sat on the edge of their seats and watched.

The Giants couldn't move the ball and punted to Baltimore soon after the overtime period began. Unitas was relentless, and the Colts moved downfield as night closed in on the game. His pinpoint pass to Raymond Berry put the ball at the Giants' 1-yard line. On the next play, Alan Ameche charged into the end zone for the winning score, making the Colts champions and forever making the NFL No. 1.

To this day, even with all the outstanding and important contests that have taken place in the NFL, that 1958 event is still known as "The Greatest Game Ever Played."

▲ Unitas signed this game-used jersey for Sports Immortals. The great quarterback was elected to the Hall of Fame in 1979; he was one of a dozen future Hall of Famers who played in the 1958 NFL Championship Game.

▲ The entire 1958 Colts championship team signed this special white football. Unitas' signature can be seen to the bottom right of the "388" marking, while Berry's is to the left.

Vince Lombardi

▲ Lombardi is featured along with star Packers running back Paul Hornung in this original painting by Ron Mahoney.

Football has always been a game for tough guys, for men who are willing to face down any odds and endure any hardship to succeed. Games in the NFL are never cancelled because of bad weather. It is never too cold or too wet or too hot to play. Pain is part of the deal.

This indomitable spirit, this desire to win no matter what the obstacle, has as its exemplar the legendary Packers coach Vince Lombardi. The former member of Fordham University's "Seven Blocks of Granite" line continued his rock-hard ways as an assistant coach in the NFL. He was named the head coach of the then-woeful Green Bay Packers in 1959 and, over the next nine years, created the greatest dynasty in league history. Lombardi's Packers won five NFL titles, as well as the first two Super Bowls.

But it was a game played on New Year's Eve 1967 that can stand as the true example of both Lombardi's leadership and of football players' willingness to withstand anything the world throws at them to play their game.

The Packers played host at Lambeau Field to the Dallas Cowboys for the NFL championship. Overnight, the temperatures had plunged so much that the heating system built into the Lambeau turf froze solid and didn't work. The thermometer read −13 and the wind-chill factor dipped to −48.

How tough was Lombardi? He went out to check the field before the

▼ Game-worn jerseys of four of Lombardi's heroes from his NFL champion Packers (clockwise from left) Jim Taylor, Forrest Gregg, Willie Davis, and Jerry Kramer.

game while still in his shirtsleeves.

The game went on, even as players were unable to dig their cleats into the frozen ground, even as lips froze and sweat crystallized. The halftime band couldn't play because they couldn't touch their frozen instruments. It was not a game, it was survival.

For a while, it looked like the visiting Cowboys would be the sole survivor, as they took a 17–14 lead late into the fourth quarter.

Lombardi exhorted his troops to come back as thousands of frozen fans added applause muffled by gloves and cheers muted by hoarse throats.

Quarterback Bart Starr, amazingly still playing without gloves, led the Packers relentlessly down the field. Finally, they reached the Dallas 1-yard line with half a minute left in the game. Calling timeout, Starr and Lombardi huddled and the quarterback thought he could sneak it over.

"Then do it and let's get the hell out of here," Lombardi famously growled.

Starr did it, following Jerry Kramer's leveling block, and the Packers earned their fifth NFL title in seven years.

Not long after adding a victory in Super Bowl II two weeks later to his list of accomplishments, Lombardi announced his retirement. He left behind a legacy of greatness, of toughness, of determination and grit that has never been matched.

▲ The game-worn jerseys of three superstar players who thrived under the harsh Lombardi rule. Starr and Nitschke survived the Ice Bowl of 1967, while Paul Hornung (No. 5) helped the Packers establish their dynasty in the first part of the 1960s.

▲ Lombardi autographed this cap, which he wore while coaching the Packers.

Super Bowl I

It might be hard for young football fans to believe, but there was a time when the Super Bowl was not the biggest single-day sporting event on the planet. In fact, the NFL was 47 years old before the first Super Bowl was played.

The creation of the game had as many twists and turns as an 80-yard punt return. In 1960 the American Football League was formed to challenge the established NFL. They were moderately successful, but by the middle of the 1960s, cooler heads realized that cooperation would work better than competition. The two leagues agreed to merge beginning with the 1970 season, but also decided to play a postseason game between each league's champion beginning after the 1966 season.

▼ This program from Super Bowl I is signed by every member of the Packers team that defeated the Chiefs.

World Championship Game AFL vs. NFL

JANUARY 15, 1967/LOS ANGELES COLISEUM   PRICE $1.00

The AFL champ that season was the Kansas City Chiefs, while the NFL title went (again) to the Green Bay Packers, one of pro football's mightiest teams ever. The two teams met in what was then called the "AFL-NFL World Championship Game." That's right: the first Super Bowl wasn't a Super Bowl at the time. (It would become the Super Bowl officially for Super Bowl III; the name came from an idea Chiefs owner Lamar Hunt had after watching his kids play with the popular toy "super ball.")

Today the Super Bowl is a worldwide spectacle watched by hundreds of millions, and tickets to the game are one of sports' hardest to obtain. But Super Bowl I, as it would later be called, was not even a sellout. The Los Angeles Coliseum was only two-thirds full at kickoff, and the game was actually blacked out in the L.A. area on both of the two networks broadcasting the game (NBC and CBS).

Coach Vince Lombardi's signature (top left) highlights the autographs on this ball, signed by the winners of the first Super Bowl.

▼ They were already champions —of the American Football League— when they played the Packers in Super Bowl I, but these Chiefs—Buck Buchanan, Willie Lanier, Len Dawson, and Bobby Bell—did not end the day as winners. Today, all are members of the Pro Football Hall of Fame.

The game also lacked the entertainment flourishes that mark today's Super spectacles, although two men wearing rocket backpacks did float into the Coliseum carrying the two game balls (each league used its own official ball on offense). The halftime entertainment was a college marching band, not a big-name entertainer.

The action on the field was not exactly memorable, either. The Chiefs trailed only 14–10 at halftime, as their powerful defense briefly held the Packers' machine in check. Two third-quarter touchdowns helped Green Bay romp in the second half, and the Packers won 35–10. The highlight for fans was the surprise success of Green Bay receiver Max McGee, who had caught only four passes all season, but was called unexpectedly into action due to an injury to starter Boyd Dowler. Off the bench McGee caught seven passes for 138 yards and two touchdowns.

Though the first Super Bowl was a relatively quiet affair, it proved the old saying: From tiny acorns grow mighty oaks.

Super Bowl III

▲ Super Bowl III hero Joe Namath signed this action photo to Joel Platt and Sports Immortals.

In Super Bowl III, David won again. The mouse conquered the lion. The kid knocked out the champ. The nag outraced the thoroughbred.

The New York Jets' epochal 16–7 victory over the Baltimore Colts was, by many accounts, the greatest and certainly most important upset in sports history. Fans who watched the game, and people who read about it today, can be inspired to know that no matter what the odds, the underdog always has a chance.

Coming into the game, the reputation of the AFL had been sullied by two straight losses to NFL champions in the postseason title game. Most fans felt that the older, established NFL would always be better than the younger, newer teams of the AFL. Further, the final agreement to the proposed merger between the two leagues may have been riding on the outcome; another disastrous defeat for the AFL team—the New York Jets this time—might have spelled the end of the union.

To make the outcome seemingly more obvious, the Colts entered the game with a 15–1 record and boasted a host of All-Pro performers; meanwhile the Jets had posted only the third-best record in the AFL that season. The oddsmakers installed the Colts as a prohibitive 17-point favorite.

Jets' quarterback Joe Namath paid little attention to all that pressure and all those predictions. He was a brash, hard-throwing passer out of the

▼ Namath's autograph (top) highlights this commemorative helmet signed by members of the Jets' Super Bowl III–winning team.

▲ Namath signed this game-used jersey to Joel Platt and Sports Immortals.

University of Alabama who signed a rich contract. A few days before the game, he made his own prediction, a statement that would become one of the most famous in sports history.

At a dinner given for the Jets, he stood up and said, "We're gonna win. I guarantee it."

The media and fans felt that Namath should have just guaranteed that he'd keep the sun from coming up. Worse, the statement galled the Colts, who had needed little additional ammunition in their zeal to beat the upstarts.

In a game that almost certainly changed the destiny of the NFL, Namath led the Jets to a 16–7 victory, the most unexpected, surprising, and influential in football, and perhaps sports history. All of a sudden, the AFL/NFL merger was a success. Namath's guarantee, and his ability to back it up, made him a superstar and brought instant attention to the Super Bowl as a sports centerpiece.

After Super Bowl III, football was forever changed. We guarantee it.

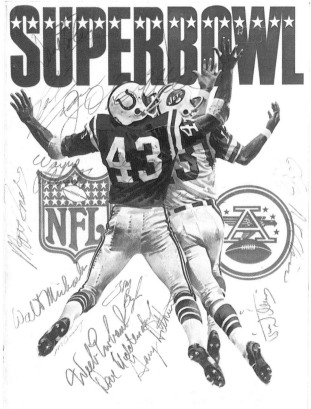

THIRD WORLD CHAMPIONSHIP GAME / JANUARY 12, 1969, ORANGE BOWL, MIAMI, FLORIDA / PRICE $1.00

▲ Members of the Jets' winning team signed this Super Bowl III program, the first to feature the words "Super Bowl" on it. Previously the game was known as the "AFL-NFL World Championship Game."

The Immaculate Reception

▲ Steelers legends Franco Harris, Lynn Swann, and Terry Bradshaw signed this photograph.

The man who had made the Pittsburgh Steelers the center of his life for nearly 40 years didn't see the most important play in the history of the franchise; he was in an elevator.

Art Rooney had founded the Steelers in 1933 and had watched his beloved team fail season after season. Heading into the 1972 season, the club had reached the playoffs only once, in 1947, and they had lost that game. But the 1972 team won the AFC Central for the first time.

The playoff game was a defensive struggle played in a packed Three Rivers Stadium. Oakland's slim 7–6 lead seemed safe as Pittsburgh faced a fourth-and-10 situation from its own 40 with 22 seconds to play.

Moments earlier, Rooney, ever the gentleman, had left the press box to go to the locker room to congratulate the Raiders. As he descended, on the field Terry Bradshaw dropped back to pass. He rifled a pass 25 yards downfield toward running back Frenchy Fuqua. The ball, Fuqua, and defender Jack Tatum all met at a point in space at the same time. The two players collided and fell to the turf, while the ball caromed backward.

▼ Harris, who signed this game-worn jersey for Sports Immortals, created a football legend by not giving up on a play at just the right moment.

Immortal Encounter

Franco Harris is a soft-spoken gentle giant whose determination and leadership led the Steelers to four Super Bowl victories. His demeanor always reminded me of Red Grange. Both were very quiet and humble off the field, but turned into tigers once the whistle blew.

I first met Franco during his rookie season with the Pittsburgh Steelers. We became instant friends and often spoke about plans for the Sports Immortals Museum. Franco indicated he would like to take an active role in helping to develop the project. Over the years he has contributed his time, effort, and several personal mementos to the Sports Immortals Museum. It's a great honor to have Franco Harris as a cochairman of the Sports Immortals Museum Honorary Board.

—Joel Platt

Rookie running back Franco Harris saw the ball tumbling toward the ground and reached out and grabbed it just before it hit the turf. He never stopped running and stormed untouched into the end zone for a miraculous touchdown.

But was it legal? The rules at the time said that if an offensive player tipped a ball, a teammate could not catch it. But if a defender hit the ball, then Harris's catch was legal. The officials huddled as the two teams and a stadium full of disbelieving fans waited.

It counted. It was a touchdown. A huge roar went up and in the elevator, Rooney asked the attendant what had happened. "I guess we scored, Mr. Rooney," the man said with a smile. The game ended a moment later with Pittsburgh a stunned and happy 13–7 victor.

The Immaculate Reception, as the catch and score came to be known, kick-started the Steelers to new heights. Two years later they won Super Bowl IX, the first of four NFL championships they would capture in the 1970s.

Art Rooney hoisted the Lombardi Trophy; he had finally seen his team on top of the mountain. This time, he didn't miss a single play.

▲ This autographed poster commemorating the first of the Steelers' four Super Bowl championships was signed by the stars of the team. Art Rooney is featured next to Franco Harris at the upper right of the artwork.

▲ These autographed jerseys were worn by three of the 10 Hall of Fame players who helped the Steelers create one of football's great dynasties. From the top, they are defensive tackle "Mean" Joe Greene, linebacker Jack Ham, and quarterback Terry Bradshaw.

▼ Franco Harris wore these cleats during his rookie season of 1972, when he gained more than 100 yards in eight consecutive games.

Walter Payton

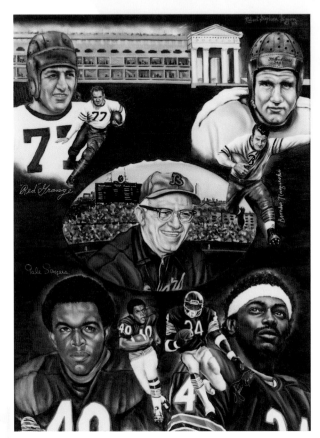

▲ Sports artist Robert Stephen Simon created this special painting to honor the Bears' great legacy of running backs. Surrounding long-time Bears coach and owner George Halas are (clockwise from top left): Red Grange, Bronko Nagurski, Walter Payton, and Gale Sayers. The painting is signed by all four runners.

When the mighty Jim Brown retired in 1965 after winning a record eight NFL rushing titles, his record of 12,312 career yards was considered almost unbreakable. Among his contemporaries and players who had preceded him, only Jim Taylor was close . . . and he was more than 3,000 yards behind.

So as the great Chicago Bears runner Walter Payton approached Brown's mark throughout the 1984 season, needing only 687 yards to top it, anticipation built and built. By the sixth game of the season, against the New Orleans Saints at Solder Field in Chicago on October 7, the man they called "Sweetness" needed only 67 yards to top Brown's 20-year-old record.

Fans and teammates alike counted down throughout the first half, but as the gun sounded, Payton was still three yards short. But on the second play of the second half, he got it, gaining six yards on a sweep around left end. Play halted as a ceremony was held on the field to recognize the NFL's new all-time rushing champion.

"Breaking Jim Brown's record," said President Ronald Reagan at the time, "is akin to Hank Aaron breaking Babe Ruth's home-run record."

But Payton, of course, did not stop there. In 1985 he was named the NFL player of the year (an honor he had also won in 1977), and helped the Bears dominate the league and win Super Bowl XX. Payton retired two years later with a grand total of 16,726 yards, a record which stood at least through the 2001 season.

While Payton's record, like Brown's, might someday fall, the great Chicago runner's place in history is assured, not only for his skill on the field, but for his

personality and
accomplishment
off it. Few play-
ers, few athletes,
few people even,
have been so
universally
liked and
admired.
Thus his illness
and death in 1999 from a rare liver disease were met with more than the nor-
mal amount of grief and sadness.

But Sweetness proved that he was a champion to
the end, bravely fighting not only for himself but
for others, as he used his name and reputation
to promote the important cause of organ
donation. Payton was taken away to enjoy
the best seat in every stadium, but the memory of his deeds, his spirit, and his life
will never fade.

▲ With a history that dates
back to the founding of the NFL,
the Chicago Bears have no
number more honored than the
No. 34 jersey of Walter
"Sweetness" Payton. This
autographed game jersey was
used by Payton in 1984,
the year he broke Jim Brown's
career rushing record.

Payton's
power
running was
key to the Bears'
Super Bowl XX
championship after the 1985
season. He and members of that
team signed this special autograph ball. ▲

Olympic Sports

▲ Clockwise from top left: 1996 torch signed by Muhammad Ali; 1960 Olympic jacket worn by Ali; 1932 and 1904 Olympic programs; 1924 Olympic vase won by swimming gold medalist Ethel Lackie; signed Carl Lewis warm-up jacket; torch signed by Al Oerter; 1936 Olympic program; photo of Jesse Owens and Luz Long; autographed Sonja Henie photo; flag signed by Maurice Greene, Marion Jones, and Michael Johnson; autographed Dream Team I cards; signed Al Oerter card; autographed Olympic stationery; Harrison Dillard race-worn shoe, with which he broke world 110-meter hurdle world record, and autographed photo.

Immortals Who Inspire

Here are stories of athletes whose achievement of character exceeded their achievements of skill.

Wilma Rudolph

No one would have faulted young Wilma Rudolph if she had never run a step. Until she was 12, she wore a brace on her withered left leg, a limb weakened by bouts with both scarlet fever and pneumonia.

But Wilma had other plans. "When that brace came off and I got on a track and ran," she once said, "I finally had the sense of saying, 'I can.'"

She certainly could. Only four years later, at the age of 16, she won a bronze medal at the 1956 Olympics in the 4x100-meter relay. She became a dominant college sprinter, and returned to the Olympics in 1960, where she became the first American woman to win three gold medals. She captured gold in the 100- and 200-meter races and led the sprint relay team to gold as well. Her feats helped her earn the Sullivan Award as the nation's top amateur athlete.

Rudolph spent her life championing the causes of young people, athletes and nonathletes alike. As an African American and as a person who overcame physical hardships, she was a prominent spokeswoman for having an inner drive to succeed.

▲ Olympic sprinter Wilma Rudolph overcame a host of obstacles to achieve her gold-medal success.

Greg Louganis

The sport of diving demands a difficult combination of strength and grace. Strength to jump, twist, spin, and flip; grace to do it with seemingly effortless ease.

In Greg Louganis, strength and grace were combined in a way never before seen in the sport. A powerful and innovative diver, he also brought a dancer's sense of style to the sport. He won a silver medal in the 1976 Montreal Olympics at the age of 16, but the United States would not return to the Olympics until 1984. He returned in triumph, winning gold in both the springboard and platform events.

Heading into the 1988 Games, Louganis was the target for every top diver in the world. No man had ever repeated in both diving events, but Louganis would give it a try. But early in the springboard competition, his Olympics, and possibly more, nearly ended when he smacked the back of his head on the springboard while doing a back flip. He plunged into the water, which was quickly tinged with his blood.

But like a hockey player, Louganis merely had the nasty cut stitched up, shook it off, and returned to the competition. Many thought he should have waited, should have not taken the risk of a worse injury. But he knew that he had only one goal: gold. And he achieved it, sweeping the two diving events with his typical flair and daring. Louganis made a tough sport look easy, and overcame a tough situation to do it.

▲ Champion diver Greg Louganis donated these signed swim trunks to Sports Immortals.

Muhammad Ali

The Olympics through the years have created dozens of emotional moments, events that bring tears to eyes around the globe.

One such came in 1996 in Atlanta, where the Games were celebrating their 100th anniversary. As the Games approached, the identity of the person who would have the honor of lighting the Olympic torch was kept top secret. Many names were batted around, but no one knew for sure until that night.

The torch was passed around the stadium by a succession of honored, well-known runners, and finally, it reached the top of the stadium, just below the cauldron towering above. Then, into the limelight that he has known more intensely than perhaps any other athlete or person, stepped Muhammad Ali.

Shaking from Parkinson's syndrome, but still the "Greatest," Ali raised the torch high and lit the flame that opened the Centennial Games. Ali's courage in his battle with infirmity simply confirmed his status as one of sports' true noblemen. The dramatic torch-lighting ceremony became another way for him to shine his unquenchable light onto the world.

Cheers and tears came in equal measure as the world saluted the champ.

▲ An autographed Olympic torch from Atlanta is framed with a signed photo of Ali in his triumphant moment; he wore the jacket when he boxed in the 1960 Olympics.

Rulon Gardner

The story is told of a little boy named David who slew a giant named Goliath armed only with a slingshot and faith.

In 2000, at the Sydney Olympic Games, David got another one.

In the world of Greco-Roman wrestling, the name of Alexander Karelin was not simply fearsome . . . it was terrifying. So powerful was the Russian wrestler that many opponents simply refused to take the mat with him, giving up their chances at championships to keep their health. Karelin was a 280-pound monster of a man whose nickname was simply the "Beast."

The heavyweight finals at Sydney paired Karelin—who had not lost in 13 years, had not allowed even a single point in 10 years, and had won nine straight world championships along with three Olympic gold medals—with Rulon Gardner, a big, smiling farm boy from Idaho.

In one of the most stunning upsets in Olympic history, Gardner refused to be cowed by Karelin's mystique. The young American, who said he built some of his strength carrying hogs on the family farm, managed to throw the Beast and earn a stunning point, and then held on doggedly against all of Karelin's charges. "I felt anything was possible with work, hard work," Gardner wrote to Sports Immortals.

At the end, the Beast was defeated, Gardner won gold, and America had a new hero, an inspiring athlete who had the faith of David.

▲ Rulon Gardner sent this autographed photo to Sports Immortals along with the secret of how he won gold.

Jim Thorpe

▼ Thorpe wrote a personal note to Joel Platt below this limited-edition lithograph, thanking him for "helping in the fight for my Olympic medals."

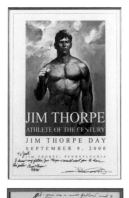

Jim Thorpe is the only Sports Immortal in this book whose accomplishments merited inclusion in two separate sections. His football deeds are outlined on pages 94–95, but it is for his Olympic success that he is perhaps more widely known.

Thorpe first made his mark in sports as a track star after serendipitously coming upon a practice at the Carlisle Indian School. Legend has it that he high-jumped nearly six feet in his overalls and was immediately signed up. He was an incredible all-around competitor, and in a 1909 meet nearly won the team title by himself.

In 1909 and 1910, however, he played a few games of summer league baseball in North Carolina, for which he was paid $18 a month. Those brief moments on the diamond would come back to cost him gold.

In 1912 Thorpe was the biggest story of the Olympics, held that summer

Immortal Encounter

In 1965 I was in California, trying to track down some Jack Dempsey items, when I realized I was just minutes from another immortal athlete, Jim Thorpe.

Thorpe's third wife, Patricia, lived in a trailer park in Banning, California. Upon arriving in Banning I called Mrs. Thorpe, and she invited me to come over. When she opened the door, I saw several elderly people inside that were bedridden and under her care.

I mentioned to Mrs. Thorpe that I had visited seven relatives of Jim Thorpe in my quest to curate his memorabilia. "Well Joel," she said, "you hit the jackpot. I have all of Jim's mementos." She got out two large boxes. The first box contained Jim's Carlisle Indians football uniform and his Canton Bulldogs uniform.

My heart began to race and my eyes got wide as she continued to pull out historical treasures. Next she held up Thorpe's Carlisle Indians football varsity sweater and at the bottom of the box she found his Sac and Fox Indian clothes and tribal garments. It was like finding King Tut's treasures. I was so in awe that I nearly forgot that she had another box.

That second box contained various trophies and medals, along with two large photo albums. The first was stamped, "Jim Thorpe's Olympic Scrapbook, Stockholm, 1912," and contained dozens of items, including rare photographs and letters from President Taft and other statesmen congratulating Jim on his Olympic success.

When I asked Mrs. Thorpe about acquiring some of Jim's items for the Sports Immortals Museum collection, she mentioned that US Steel had paid her $500 to use Jim's photo in an advertisement. I replied that I would be glad to compensate her for any items we could possibly obtain. Mrs. Thorpe said she would consider my request and to stay in touch. Over the next five years I spoke to Mrs. Thorpe numerous times and visited her on two other occasions. In 1970, more than five years after my initial visit, I received the following telegram:

"Come and get Jim's things, am confined to bed. Patricia Thorpe."

I honored her request and obtained all of Jim Thorpe's significant mementos.

—JOEL PLATT

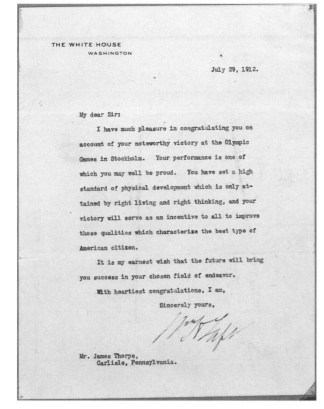

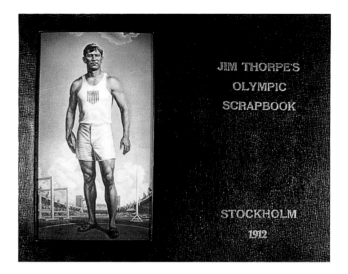

▲ Among the items contained in this 1912 Olympic scrapbook personally created by Thorpe is this personal letter from President William Howard Taft (left) congratulating the Native-American champion on his double gold-medal success in Stockholm.

in Stockholm. On July 7 he won the five-event pentathlon, contested on a single day. Later that week, he competed in the long jump and high jump but didn't medal. A few days later came the decathlon.

The grueling two-day event is the ultimate test of athletic skill, combining running, jumping, and throwing events. The winner of the quadrennial Olympic competition is regarded as the world's best athlete.

Thorpe squashed the competition, winning by an enormous 688 points. His world record 8,412 points would have been good enough for a silver medal 36 years later. Handing Thorpe the gold medal, King Gustav V of Sweden declared, "Sir, you are the greatest athlete in the world."

The very unworldly Thorpe is alleged to have replied, "Thanks, King."

Thorpe's naivete about the ways of the world would sadly blemish for generations his reputation and gold-medal status. A year after his Olympic glory, his pro baseball past was discovered, and the International Olympic Committee unceremoniously stripped him of his medals and championships.

Nearly 60 years would pass before Thorpe's medals would be "returned" to him. Unfortunately, Thorpe himself had died in 1953, not long after being named the greatest athlete of the half-century. More than that, many experts feel that Thorpe was the greatest all-around athlete in history.

▲ Thorpe received this medal for being a member of the U.S. Olympic team in 1912.

Johnny Weissmuller

He is more well known for what he did in the trees, but Johnny Weissmuller first gained international fame for what he did in the water.

Nearly 50 years before Mark Spitz made a splash in the Olympics and became an international swimming star, Weissmuller was filling the headlines with his deeds in the pool. Born in Hungary and raised in Chicago, he did not begin competitive swimming until 1920, when he was 16, but he was a national sprint champion a year later. He continued his success with national titles in 1922 and 1923.

In the 1924 Olympics in Paris, Weissmuller dominated the swimming competition, winning gold medals in the 100- and 400-meter freestyle events. He also anchored the winning 800-meter freestyle relay and even tacked on a bronze medal for his play with the water polo team.

In 1928 in Amsterdam, he continued his success, matching his gold in the 100 and earning another relay championship.

Weissmuller left the amateur ranks soon after and became a popular pitchman for BVD swimwear. But he found his greatest success and fame away from the pool when he was given the role of Tarzan in the movies. His trademark yell echoed through a dozen successful Tarzan stories from 1932 to 1948; in fact, the yell was so good that it was used on tape for many future Tarzans. One legend says he used the jungle yell to escape from bandits while on a tour of Cuba in the 1950s.

But while the general public remembers him in a loincloth, the sporting world knows that

▲ This rare statue of Weissmuller was created for the 1933 World's Fair, held in Chicago.

Weissmuller made an indelible mark on swimming, setting 51 world records in distances from 50 to 800 yards. He also set a record for a three-mile, open-water swim. Imagine sprint star Michael Johnson setting his 200-meter records and then coming back the next week to set a mark in the 1,500 and you get an idea of Weissmuller's versatility and overall dominance of swimming.

In 1950 the Associated Press named him the greatest swimmer of the half-century; most movie buffs also give him the title of the greatest movie Tarzan.

Opponents knew to call him only one thing: winner.

▲ Weissmuller himself autographed this copy of the biography that told the story of the great swimming and film star.

▲ Weissmuller was one of the first athletes to enjoy commercial success. This is a signed reprint of an ad for a life insurance company.

▲ This program is from the 1928 Olympic tryouts, at which Weissmuller continued his dominance.

Jesse Owens

▲ Jesse Owens' personal scrapbook from his Olympic trip to Germany includes snapshots of prewar Berlin and autographs from every champion from the 1936 Games.

It's one thing to outrace your opponents on the track. It's quite another to outrun evil. But that's what Jesse Owens did at the 1936 Olympics, and he beat track opponents and national enemies handily in one of the most courageous performances in sports history.

On a track surrounded by stormtroopers and Nazi banners and under the watchful, hateful eye of Adolf Hitler, who had led his followers in calling the African-American athletes less than human, Owens sprinted past hate and leaped over racism. He won gold medals in the 100- and 200-meter sprints, set a world record while winning the long jump, and anchored a gold medal–winning, record-setting 4x100-meter relay team.

The myth of the Nazi master race was ground into the cinders beneath Owens' spiked shoes.

The son of Alabama sharecroppers, Owens spent much of his youth picking cotton. His athletic talents took him away from the fields, however, and he excelled at Ohio State, winning all 42 events he entered in his junior year. His finest

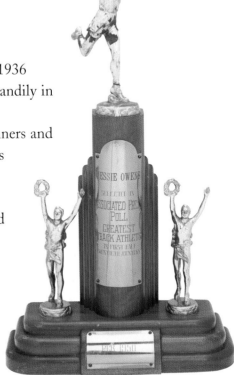

▲ Owens won this trophy in 1950 after being named the top track athlete of the half century.

Immortal Encounter

I visited Jesse and his wife at their lakefront apartment in Chicago in 1965. Because he was involved in a variety of youth programs, Jesse was excited about my ambition. He understood my vision, and saw it as an inspiration to youngsters and adults alike.

Jesse had become a polished motivational speaker and was passionate about his Olympic experiences. When I asked him about the time Adolf Hitler refused to shake his hand after Owens won his events, Jesse smiled and said quietly, "Joel, I didn't go to Berlin to shake hands with der Fuhrer."

One situation that did frustrate him about the Games was that of Marty Glickman, his teammate on the U.S. relay team. Before the relay finals, Glickman was removed from the squad after the Germans objected to him because of his Jewish faith.

After discussing Jesse's career for almost half an hour, the conversation returned to the museum. Jesse told me that he had several items that he wanted to donate to the collection, and asked if I would come back the following day. When I returned, Mrs. Owens said that her husband had been called away on a last-minute speaking engagement, but that she had all the items Jesse promised.

Jesse had provided a beautiful trophy he won for being chosen greatest track athlete of the first half of the 20th century; a personal photo album of prewar Germany autographed by every champion from the 1936 Olympic Games; an Olympic bell that Jesse had been given; and a plaque Jesse had won at Cleveland's Fairmount Junior High School.

—JOEL PLATT

◄ A medal from the 1936 Olympic Games. Note the German imperial eagle below the ribbon and above the Olympic rings.

OLYMPIC GAMES 1936.

▼▲ A program from the Games that Owens made his own. The ceramic bell below was given to Owens in Berlin.

hour before Berlin came in the 1935 Big Ten Championships, when he set three world records and tied another in the span of just 45 minutes.

Though Owens was favored to do well at the Berlin Olympics the following year, he was under enormous pressure, running in front of the symbols that would soon spread evil over Europe. But he persevered, dominating the competition. He was received as a hero back in the United States but, in a sad irony of the times, was still treated as a second-class citizen.

"When I came back home, I couldn't ride in the front of the bus," Owens said. "I couldn't live where I wanted. I wasn't invited to shake hands with Hitler, but I wasn't invited to the White House to shake hands with the president, either."

He suffered some hard times, but by the 1950s, he was more fully recognized for his awesome achievements, and was voted the top track athlete of the half century. In 1976 he received the Presidential Medal of Freedom.

The man who outran evil passed away in 1980. Owens remains to this day an enduring symbol of the power of one man to help right a great wrong. His courage is an inspiration for future generations to follow his lead.

Mark Spitz

mark spitz

arena

▲ An autographed photo of Mark Spitz with his incredible display of seven gold medals.

Athletes often must deal with massive hype and inflated expectations. The press, fans, and their peers—and in some cases, themselves—all combine to build up to a potential that, when not met, is seen as a failure rather than as a success on its own merits.

When Mark Spitz arrived in Munich for the 1972 Olympics, he carried around his neck the label of "unfulfilled potential." He was a child prodigy swimming star, the best in the nation in his age group at 10 years old. He won five medals at the 1967 Pan Am Games and 24 AAU titles. But in 1968 at the Mexico City Games, he had won only two team golds when he had expected to win many more.

Four years later, the expectations were even higher. Three times after Mexico City he had been named Swimmer of the Year, and he had won the 1971 Sullivan Award as the nation's top amateur athlete. Anything but a handful of golds would have seemed a disappointment.

But remarkably, showing the inner drive that makes true champions, Spitz exceeded even the loftiest of predictions. In just over a week, Spitz won an all-time record seven gold medals, in the process setting or helping set seven world records. No Olympic athlete in any sport, before or since, has matched his record in a single Games.

He first won, in order, the 200 butterfly, the 200 freestyle, the 100 butterfly, and the 100 freestyle. As if that wasn't enough, he was part of gold medal–winning relay teams in the 4x100 freestyle, 4x200 freestyle, and 4x100 medley relay.

▲ This is one of the 1972 Olympic torches that carried the flame to Munich to shine above Spitz's achievements.

Seven gold medals. A stunning achievement, but it was put in grim perspective just days later by the actions of Palestinian terrorists who kidnapped Israeli athletes. Sadly, all the hostages were killed in a rescue attempt undertaken by West German authorities.

Spitz was taken to safety by American officials who feared that his status as a hero and his Jewish heritage might make him a target.

Though the Munich Games remain blanketed in sorrow for the tragic events, the shining gold medals around Mark Spitz's neck remain for all time a symbol of individual success.

To Joel,
My Greatest Moment
was winning Seven
Gold Medals at the
20th Olympic Games
in Germany
Best Wishes
Mark Spitz

▲ Not surprisingly, Spitz wrote to Sports Immortals that his seven 1972 gold medals collectively were his greatest moment in sports.

▲ Spitz autographed his personal swim trunks when donating them to the Sports Immortals collection.

Dorothy Hamill

American women have always played a big part in Olympic ice skating competitions. Tenley Albright, Carol Heiss, and Peggy Fleming all captured Olympic gold and the hearts of their country. More recently, Kristi Yamaguchi and Sarah Hughes have captured gold on ice. But in 1976 a skater blew away the competition and became America's sweetheart of the ice in a way not truly seen before or since. Combining fluid skating, grace, and a haircut that was almost as famous as she was, Dorothy Hamill was a golden winter princess.

Growing up in Connecticut, Hamill followed her hockey-playing brothers onto the ice; she actually had to stuff socks into the toes of their larger skates to give skating a try. She fell in love with it at once and soon became a regular at national competitions. Her finest moment came in Innsbruck, Austria, at the 1976 Winter Games.

▲ The dazzlingly beautiful and equally talented Sonja Henie of Norway was perhaps the greatest Olympic ice skater ever, male or female. Here she appears in a publicity shot from one of the many movies she made after her skating career ended.

Sonja Henie

While Dorothy Hamill represents the modern skating champion, she still has a long way to go to match Sonja Henie's worldwide acclaim.

The Norwegian beauty first competed in the Olympics in 1924 when she was only 11. She returned in 1928 to win the first of her three consecutive gold medals. She remains the only three-time champion in figure skating, male or female. Trained in ballet, she combined artistry, beauty, and technical elegance in a way never before seen. Along with winning a stunning 10 straight world championships, she single-handedly made figure skating a premier Olympic event. After her athletic career ended, she parlayed her Olympic fame into a successful career as a leading actress in Hollywood movies and traveling ice shows.

After her final free skate, she was put in first place by all nine judges. Her unaffected personality and all-American beauty combined to make her a national darling. Her unique wedge-shaped haircut immediately became an enormous hit, too. Fashion experts later called it one of the most influential fashion icons of the century.

Wearing a bright pink outfit trimmed in white, Hamill flawlessly skated through her final program, utilizing an artistry rarely seen on the ice combined with the unique Hamill Camel move.

"I remember most the flowers floating down on the ice after I finished," she told CNNSI.com in 2001. "And, of course, standing on the podium with that great sense of pride of being an American and having achieved a goal I had."

After winning the world championship the following year, she became a professional skater and continued to capture championships. She moved on to become one of the top touring acts in the world of ice skating entertainment, while continuing to be a well-loved spokesperson for both commerical products and the many charities she supports.

The little girl in the over-sized skates had become an international superstar.

▼ Below is Dorothy Hamill's ice skating costume and skates. Dorothy's accomplishments are among the the great all-American success stories in Olympic history.

The 1980 U.S. Hockey Team

Rare is the sports event that enters the consciousness of an entire nation and is talked about, remembered, and loved by everyone, sports fan and non–sports fan alike. Such a moment occurred during the ice hockey competition of the 1980 Winter Olympics. The Cold War was still on and America and the Soviet Union were still bitter enemies; months later, the United States would boycott the Summer Olympics in protest of the USSR's invasion of Afghanistan.

The Soviets were dominant in ice hockey, having won every Olympic ice hockey gold medal but one since 1956. The U.S. team, meanwhile, was made up of college players, many of them not even 21 years old. Early in the Games, the hometown fans in Lake Placid, New York, helped the U.S. build a surprising 3–0–1 record in early competition, leading to a showdown with the USSR.

After two periods the game was tight, but the Soviets led 3–2. The third period, however, was all U.S. Mark Johnson tied the score midway through the period. And then, with just over 10 minutes remaining, captain Mike Eruzione scored on a slapshot to give the U.S. its first lead of the game.

The noise was deafening inside the arena in Lake Placid as the young American team held off dozens of furious rushes from the veteran Soviets, who had won the last 21 Olympic hockey games they had played. Goalie Jim Craig made several brilliant saves, and the crowd screamed at every close play.

▼ This special commemorative poster was signed by all 20 members of the gold medal–winning team.

Remember the Moment

XIII WINTER OLYMPIC GAMES
LAKE PLACID, N.Y. U.S.A. ★ FEBRUARY 22 & 24, 1980

USA 4   USSR 3   USA 4   FINLAND 2

◄ This 1980 U.S. Olympic hockey team jersey (the No. 30 is for goalie Jim Craig) is signed by the entire team. It is framed with commemorative covers of *Sports Illustrated* published after the victory over the Soviet Union (center) and naming the team the "Sportsmen of the Year" (bottom right).

But the Soviet team could not break the American's defenses . . . or their will.

As the seconds ticked down to zero, Al Michaels, calling the game for ABC Sports, yelled out the famous call that has come to stand for that victory. As the players poured onto the ice to celebrate, Michaels said simply, "Do you believe in miracles? YES!"

The victory touched every part of America. Stories were told of restaurant patrons standing and singing, of hospitals putting TVs into emergency rooms so doctors could watch, of high school gymnasiums standing and applauding when the score was announced.

But what most people don't remember is that the epic victory did not guarantee the Americans a gold medal. They still had to defeat Finland two days later to earn their Olympic title, and they had to pull off another amazing comeback to do it. But their 3–2 victory in that game gave them a totally unexpected and nation-rousing gold medal.

Other Sports

▲ Clockwise from top left: helmet and racing gloves used by Al Unser in an Indy 500; Teofilo Cubillas soccer game jersey; helmet worn by Jorge Velasquez when he rode Pleasant Colony to victory in the Kentucky Derby; Dale Earnhardt signed die-cast car; Bobby Hull game jersey; whip used by Laffit Pincay Jr.; giant tennis ball signed by Bjorn Borg and other champions; 1954 soccer program signed by Sir Stanley Mathews; puck autographed by Mario Lemieux; putter used by Patty Berg; early golf glove worn by Chick Evans.

129

Immortals Who Inspire

Here are stories of athletes whose achievement of character exceeded their achievements of skill.

Ben Hogan

▲ Golfing legend Ben Hogan autographed this head cover for a number-four wood.

Golfer Ben Hogan and his wife were a couple of hours east of El Paso in 1949, driving a two-lane country highway en route to a tournament in Arizona, when disaster struck. A bus traveling the opposite direction pulled out of its lane to pass a slow-moving truck and plowed head-on into the couple's car.

Hogan had little time to react behind the wheel, but threw himself in front of his wife to protect her. As it turned out, she suffered only minor injuries in the wreck. Hogan was not as fortunate. He had multiple injuries, including a broken collarbone, ankle, and rib, and two fractures of his pelvis. The broken bones would heal and an operation saved him from a potentially fatal blood clot, but there was little doubt among the doctors who cared for him: Hogan would never play golf again.

Hogan, however, had other ideas. His indomitable will had often carried him to victory even when his game was not its sharpest, and now he called upon that will to sustain him in the greatest challenge of his life.

He had been the leading money winner on the PGA Tour three times in the early 1940s before joining the army, and he not only made it all the way back to that peak, he was as good as ever. Only 16 months after the accident, Hogan won the 1950 U.S. Open.

Though effects from the accident curtailed the number of events he entered during the rest of his career, Hogan successfully defended that title in 1951. He won his fourth Open two years later, when he also won the Masters and the British Open. In all, he had nine major titles among his 63 tournament victories, both figures third-best of all-time. But perhaps his most important achievement was coming back from his terrible injuries. The greatest athletes ignore the naysayers and strive for success, no matter the odds.

Mario Lemieux

Hockey superstar Mario Lemieux retired following the 1996–1997 season with 613 goals and 1,494 points while playing 745 games in 13 seasons with the NHL's Pittsburgh Penguins. Those are excellent numbers, Hall-of-Fame numbers, in fact. And indeed, Lemieux was inducted into the Hockey Hall of Fame that year.

But three years later, in late December 2000, with the Penguins struggling on the ice and at the gate, Lemieux stepped out of the club's front office and back into his uniform. He practiced with the team for the first time on December 19, then played his first game against Toronto on December 27. That night he scored a goal and had two assists. He went on to score 35 goals and tally 76 points in only 45 games.

That Lemieux could make such an effortless return to the ice at age 35 and after three years away surprised few hockey observers. After all, they had already seen it before, when Lemieux overcame a battle with Hodgkin's disease.

Lemieux missed a month of the 1992–1993 season while undergoing radiation treatment for the cancer, yet still earned one of his six Hart Trophies as the league's leading scorer, totaling 160 points in only 60 games. Throughout much of the 1990s, Lemieux also battled serious back problems, and even sat out the 1994–1995 season. He led the league again by scoring 161 points in 70 games during the 1995–1996 season. Few athletes reach such heights of success, fewer still while overcoming such serious illness and injury.

Lemieux's physical battles are heartwarming enough, but he also endeared himself to Penguins fans forever by saving the franchise twice from near financial ruin. The first time came in 1984–1985, when his arrival as a highly touted rookie revived interest and increased attendance. Then in 1999 he took over ownership of the franchise and kept the club in Pittsburgh. Super Mario, indeed.

▲ A signed, game-used jersey from Mario Lemieux, one of hockey's greatest scorers and most inspirational heroes.

Lance Armstrong

Let's face it, sometimes it doesn't take much for a lot of us to be stopped by life's little roadblocks. Got the sniffles? Call in sick to work. A sore back? Sorry, dear, no chores today. I'll watch TV from the couch.

In 1996 Lance Armstrong was near the peak of his profession, ranked among the top 10 professional cyclists in the world, when he ran into a major road block: he was diagnosed with advanced testicular cancer that had spread to his lungs and his brain.

Armstrong knew he was facing an uphill climb more treacherous than a mountain stage of the Tour de France. But he attacked the disease with a determination characteristic of his performance on the race course. Three operations and the most aggressive chemotherapy available were successful, and he began training again only five months after the original diagnosis.

Armstrong already was one of the most successful American cyclists in history. But after returning to his bike, he worked harder than ever to become one of the most successful cyclists in the world. In 1999 he won the grueling Tour de France, the world's premier cycling event. He successfully defended that title a year later, then made it three consecutive victories in 2001.

After his illness, Armstrong began riding for the United States Postal Service Pro Cycling team. That was appropriate because the postal carrier's creed is the familiar "Neither rain, nor sleet, nor snow . . . will keep us from our appointed rounds." Not even a battle with cancer was going to keep Lance Armstrong from his destiny.

▲ A signed racing jersey from cyclist Lance Armstrong, who overcame cancer to become one of America's premier international athletes.

Bobby Jones

Great athletes often talk about the need to know when to walk away from the game. Few ever walked away at the absolute apex of their career. Golfer Bobby Jones did.

In September 1930 Jones won the U.S. Amateur Championship. Because he had already won the British Open, the British Amateur, and the U.S. Open that year, Jones' victory gave him an unprecedented Grand Slam. Two months later, at age 28, he retired from competitive golf.

Jones was a child prodigy who was winning club championships by the time he was 12 and qualified for his first U.S. Amateur at 14. But until he was 21, he didn't fulfill the vast potential of his teenage years. Then, in 1923, Jones broke through to win the U.S. Open. That victory began a remarkable string of 13 championships in 20 majors. He won the U.S. Amateur five times, the U.S. Open four times, the British Open three times, and the British Amateur once.

Still, golf was not an all-consuming element of Jones' life. Though on the course he was one of the fiercest competitors that the game has ever seen, he was never more than a part-time player. While amassing his major titles, he also was busy earning bachelor's degrees in mechanical engineering from Georgia Tech and English literature from Harvard, and also a law degree at Emory.

He retired from golf to practice law, though he remained in the sport by founding the Augusta National Golf Club in 1933. One

▲ This one-of-a-kind doll was created for display at the 1933 World's Fair in Chicago.

Golf

year later, Augusta hosted its first Masters.

A spinal disease first diagnosed in 1948 eventually left Jones confined to a wheelchair and ultimately led to his death in 1971. His courage while facing this challenge was as inspirational as his play on the golf course.

Jones was a charter inductee of the World Golf Hall of Fame in 1974.

Things have changed over the years. The Masters and the PGA Championship have replaced the British and U.S. Amateur Championships among golf's majors. Jack Nicklaus came along and broke Jones's career record for major titles. More recently, Tiger Woods won all four majors in succession.

But Jones remains the lone golfer to complete the Grand Slam in one season.

▼ Jones himself donated this sportsmanship medal for display in the Sports Immortals Museum.

◄ This display includes three of Bobby Jones' golf clubs and an autographed photo of the great champion.

Babe Didrikson Zaharias

▲ Autobiography of Babe Didrikson Zaharias signed by Babe and her husband George.

At the 1932 Olympics in Los Angeles, 18-year-old Babe Didrikson entered three events, the maximum allowed for women. She won the javelin throw with a world-record toss, won the 80-meter hurdles in world-record time, and apparently won the gold medal in the high jump with a world-record leap, only to have a controversial disqualification relegate her to second place.

There was nothing Didrikson couldn't do on an athletic field. Prior to the Olympics, she carried her club to the team title at the national AAU Track and Field Championships in 1932—even though she was the club's lone entry. She was a basketball star, and was accomplished in tennis, bowling, volleyball, and just about any other sport at which she tried. She once pitched an inning in a major league baseball spring training game. In another exhibition, she reportedly struck out the Yankees' Joe DiMaggio.

But it was on golf that Didrikson eventually concentrated. According to the legend, famed sportswriter Grantland Rice joined Didrikson during the 1932 Olympics for a friendly game of golf at the local Brentwood Country Club. A newcomer to golf, Didrikson could hit the ball so far that Rice convinced her to take up the sport seriously. And from then on, she dominated golf like no other woman before or since.

Didrikson was declared a professional in 1935 because of an unauthorized endorsement, but had her amateur status reinstated in 1943, by which time she was married to George Zaharias, a pro wrestler. From 1946–1947, she won 17 consecutive tournaments, and turned professional after becoming the first American to win the British Ladies' Amateur Championship in the summer of 1947.

▲ Legendary champion Bobby Jones gave this 9-iron to Zaharias, who used it in several tournaments during her record-setting golf career.

Golf

▲ The greatest woman golfer of the first half of the 20th century, Babe Zaharias poses here with trophies she took home for winning the United States open (left) and British Ladies' Amateur Championship.

◄ Babe Zaharias also used this wooden-shafted putter.

Didrikson was known as much for her indomitable will as for her natural athletic ability and tireless work ethic (she would hit as many as 1,000 golf balls a day). Her will was never more evident than during the summer of 1953, when she returned to competition less than four months after cancer surgery. The next year, she lapped the field at the U.S. Women's Open, winning by 12 strokes. She won five tournaments that year and was named the *Associated Press* female athlete of the year for the sixth time.

In 1956 Babe died of cancer at age 42, but her achievements will never be forgotten.

With my Best

Mildred "Babe" Zaharias

◄ Though golf was her greatest sport, Zaharias was one of the most multitalented athletes of all time, male or female. Here she shows off the hurdling form that helped her win gold in the 1932 Olympics. Her autograph, including her famous nickname, is below.

Jack Nicklaus

A 30 on the back nine anywhere is worthy of note. A 30 on the back nine at Augusta in the final round of The Masters is cause for celebration.

So when Jack Nicklaus walked up to the 18th green at the 1986 Masters, the gallery erupted in a deafening ovation. It wasn't just that Nicklaus was a crowd favorite who had won the green jacket five previous times. It was also that Nicklaus was 46 at the time, and few people believed that he could muster the skill to win a sixth title.

But grit and determination were as much the hallmarks of the "Golden Bear" as physical ability. And when Nicklaus' tap-in for par on the 18th stood up for a one-stroke victory over Greg Norman and Tom Kite, he became the oldest player ever to win a major championship.

By almost any statistical measure, Nicklaus is one of the greatest golfers ever to play the game. He was an eight-time PGA player of the year and was the leading money winner on the tour eight times. He won 70 PGA tournaments, then 10 more on the senior tour. During the prime of his career from 1962 through 1979, he finished among the top 10 in two of every three tournaments he entered. He was undefeated while playing for two Walker Cup teams, and won 17 matches for eight Ryder Cup teams in competition against Europe.

▲ Nicklaus enjoyed the cheers of the gallery after he won his record sixth Masters in 1986.

▲ Nicklaus autographed these golf spikes, which he wore during his amazing career.

▲ Is there a more classic moment in golf than Jack Nicklaus achingly standing frozen for what seems like forever over a clutch putt . . . and then sinking it? Nicklaus used this putter to do just that in several major tournaments.

But the one measure that truly sets Nicklaus apart is the one that matters most to him: his record 20 major championship titles.

As a youngster growing up in his native Ohio in the 1940s and 1950s, Nicklaus idolized the legendary Bobby Jones, who then held the record with 13 major championships. Nicklaus would eventually shatter that mark by winning his 14th major title at the PGA Championship in 1973. It was the third of his five PGA crowns. He also won The Masters six times, the U.S. Open four times, the British Open three times, and the U.S. Amateur twice.

▲ This bronze of Jack Nicklaus was cast to celebrate the centennial of golf in America.

▲ Masters hat autographed by golf immortals Jack Nicklaus, Arnold Palmer, and Tiger Woods.

▼ Before metal woods, titanium shafts, and high-tech iron designs, Nicklaus used this plain old wood driver in many wonderful ways. His strength and length off the tee were a big part of his early success.

Arnold Palmer

Trailing leader Ken Venturi by one stroke in the final round of the 1960 Masters at Augusta, Arnold Palmer rolled in a lengthy birdie putt on the 17th hole to pull even. Another birdie on 18 gave Palmer the green jacket.

It was the type of dramatic victory that is the achievement of a golfer's lifetime. But it turns out that Palmer was just warming up.

Two months later Palmer entered the final round of the U.S. Open at Cherry Hills in Colorado a whopping seven shots and 14 places behind leader Mike Souchak. Palmer birdied six of the first seven holes, went on to shoot 65, and won the tournament by two shots.

The two major titles epitomized the come-from-behind charge that the legions of "Arnie's Army" would come to expect and enjoy for years to come. Before he stopped playing regularly on the PGA Tour, Palmer won 60 events, including The Masters four times and the British Open twice. He played on seven Ryder Cup teams, was the leading money winner on tour four times, and was named the PGA player of the year twice. He was the first to win $1 million in career earnings, and his battles with an up-and-coming young star in the 1960s, Jack Nicklaus, were epic.

In 1980 Palmer energized the Senior Tour and delighted his army as he had done on the PGA Tour. He won the Senior PGA Championship in the first event he entered, and won nine more events in his senior career.

▼ We're in the army now: A golf ball autographed by Arnold Palmer, leader of the legion of fans known as "Arnie's Army."

▲ Palmer donated this putter and iron used in winning several tournaments to the Sports Immortals Collection.

LEGENDS ON THE SWILKEN BRIDGE
1995 • ARNIE'S LAST BRITISH OPEN
ST. ANDREWS • SCOTLAND

▲ Palmer (red shirt) posed with Raymond Floyd, Tom Watson, and Jack Nicklaus on the Swilken Bridge at St. Andrew's during Palmer's final British Open appearance in 1995. Below the photos are autographed first-day issue postcards of each golfer.

But Palmer's influence extends far beyond the statistics. Charismatic and energetic, he helped bring golf to the masses, and captivated new fans lured to the game by television. Off the course, he became a successful businessman and golf ambassador whose appeal has outlived his days near the top of the leaderboard.

▲ This limited-edition bronze of Palmer's famous swing was created to celebrate the centennial of golf in America.

Arnold Palmer
Golfer of the Decade 1958-1967
Centennial of Golf in America

Immortal Encounter

In sports, Latrobe, Pennsylvania, has two great distinctions. The first professional football game was played in Latrobe in 1865. It is also the birthplace of Arnold Palmer, one of the greatest golfers of all time.

In the late 1950s I was traveling to Somerset, Pennsylvania, for a business meeting. Driving on Route 30 from Pittsburgh I passed through Latrobe and saw a sign indicating the city was the birthplace of Arnold Palmer. After pulling into a gas station, I was told that the Palmers lived near the grounds of the Latrobe Country Club. Ten minutes later I entered the long

driveway leading to Arnold Palmer's residence. It was my lucky day: Arnie was working on some golf clubs in a workshop behind his house. He was famous for modifying his personal clubs and had several hundred lined up in the workshop. After speaking with Arnie for 30 minutes about my museum project, I inquired about obtaining some of his personal mementos. He presented me two clubs he used in winning several tournaments along with a beautiful autographed photo.

—JOEL PLATT

Bobby Orr

The image is the most famous in the history of hockey, one of the most famous in all of sports: Bobby Orr (right) flying through the air in front of the net, feet off the ground, parallel to the ice with arms outstretched in triumph. In the background, distraught St. Louis Blues players are juxtaposed with jubilant Boston Garden fans.

Orr had just scored the winning goal in overtime of the fourth and final game of the 1970 Stanley Cup Finals, breaking a 3–3 tie and lifting the Boston Bruins to a four-game sweep and their first National Hockey League title in 29 years.

Bobby Orr was just 22 at the time of his Stanley Cup–winning goal, but it was the defining moment in the career of a player who revolutionized his position and the sport.

Orr began playing organized hockey at age five in his native Parry Sound, Ontario, Canada, and by thirteen had signed a junior contract with Boston. He entered the NHL in 1966 at 18 and was named the league's top rookie the following spring. The next year, he won the first of eight consecutive Norris Trophies as the top defenseman in the league. But he did it in unconventional fashion, attacking the net, scoring goals, and amassing points at a prolific pace.

In 1970 Orr led the league with 120 points, the first time a defenseman ever won the scoring crown and the first of his six

▼ He shoots . . . he scores! Bruins win! Bobby Orr goes flying into history after scoring the Stanley Cup–winning goal in Game 4 of the 1970 Finals. He autographed this photo, perhaps the most famous ever taken of NHL action.

▼ No fiberglass for Bobby Orr, as shown by this autographed wooden hockey stick, which he used during his incredible career.

consecutive 100-point seasons. He led the league in scoring again in 1975, when he had a career-high 46 goals en route to 135 points.

A three-time recipient of the Hart Memorial Trophy as the NHL's most valuable player, Orr was also named the MVP of the playoffs in 1970 and 1972 (he led the Bruins to a Stanley Cup victory in six games over the New York Rangers in 1972). He played 10 years for Boston, then finished his career by playing parts of injury-plagued seasons in 1976–1977 and 1978–1979 with the Chicago Blackhawks.

At 31 in 1979, Orr became the youngest player ever inducted into the Hockey Hall of Fame.

▲ The most famous defenseman in hockey wore these home and away Bruins jerseys and autographed them for Sports Immortals.

Gordie Howe

▲ The man they call "Mr. Hockey" signed this photo taken after he scored his then-record 600th NHL goal for Detroit.

At 52, most people are quietly counting the days until they begin drawing on their retirement accounts or pensions. Only one man was still mixing it up on the boards and shooting the puck on the net in the National Hockey League at that age, and that was Gordie Howe.

In 1979–1980, Howe played his 26th, and final, season in the NHL for the Hartford Whalers. Add in six seasons in the World Hockey Association, and Howe played 32 years of major league hockey— a record for longevity that likely will never be broken.

But Howe is not remembered simply for his endurance. One of the smartest and toughest players in hockey history, he won six Hart Memorial Trophies as the NHL's most valuable player, and was a first- or second-team All-Star a remarkable 21 times.

In 1946 Howe scored a goal in his first game as an 18-year-old rookie. By the time he retired 34 years later (he also spent two seasons as a Red Wings executive from 1972–1973 before returning to the ice in the WHA), "Mr. Hockey" had established NHL records for goals, assists, points, and games played. He won six scoring titles, and finished

▲ The only two-generation line in hockey history wore these jerseys with the Houston Aeros of the WHA.

Hockey

among the league's top five scorers for 20 consecutive seasons from 1950–1969. More importantly, he led his NHL teams to the playoffs 20 times, and helped the Red Wings to four Stanley Cup titles between 1950 and 1955.

At age 45 in 1973, Howe left the executive offices of the Red Wings to play with sons Mark and Marty on the Houston Aeros of the newly formed WHA. The Aeros won the first two league titles with the three Howes leading the way. Later, Mark joined Gordie in his final NHL season with the Whalers. Marty was called up from the minors to join them, too.

But even after retiring in 1980, Gordie Howe went back on the ice one last time. In 1997, at age 69, Howe played a shift with the International League's Detroit Vipers to mark the sixth decade in which he skated as a pro.

The most remarkable career in hockey had come to a close, but Howe had created a legend that will never die.

▲ This signed, game-worn jersey is an example of the famous No. 9 that Gordie Howe wore while helping the Red Wings win four Stanley Cup championships.

▲ One of the game sticks used by Gordie Howe during his NHL career. Howe scored a total of 801 NHL goals.

Wayne Gretzky

As a youngster, Wayne Gretzky originally wanted to wear uniform No. 9 like his idol, NHL Hall of Famer Gordie Howe. In the end, he had to settle for 99—which was appropriate because what he accomplished on the ice far surpassed the exploits even of the legendary "Mr. Hockey."

▲ Gretzky signed and donated the hockey stick he used in the 1981 NHL All-Star Game to Sports Immortals .

▲ This pennant, signed by Gretzky, celebrates his greatest season. In 1981–1982, he not only led the Edmonton Oilers to the Stanley Cup title, he also set records with 92 goals and 120 assists for a total of 212 points.

From the time Gretzky scored 378 goals in one season as a 10-year-old in Brantford, Ontario, in 1971 until he retired from the NHL holding 61 league records in 1999, Gretzky had no peer on the ice. His laundry list of feats can go on and on. Nine Hart Memorial Trophies in a 10-year span as the NHL's most valuable player; 10 league scoring crowns; the only four 200-point regular seasons in league history; more goals, assists, and points than any other player in history; All-Star selections in each season of his 20-year career; and four Stanley Cup titles in a five-year stretch with the Edmonton Oilers, 1984–1988.

Gretzky's 92 goals for the Oilers in 1981–1982 were to hockey what Barry Bonds' 73 home runs would be to baseball in 2001. Gretzky's mark was stunning because it shattered Phil Esposito's seemingly unreachable mark of 76 goals, set 11 seasons earlier, just as Bonds outdistanced Mark McGwire's 70 homers in 1998.

Still, for all of his ability to put the puck into the net, Gretzky was primarily a playmaker, an instinc-

▲ This hand-painted hockey puck by Yuri Liaboh features a portrait of Gretzky during his years with the Los Angeles Kings.

Hockey

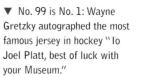

▼ No. 99 is No. 1: Wayne Gretzky autographed the most famous jersey in hockey "To Joel Platt, best of luck with your Museum."

▼ The greatest career in hockey history made stops in four places. This autographed display shows Gretzky with (clockwise from top left) the Oilers, the Kings, the Blues, and the Rangers.

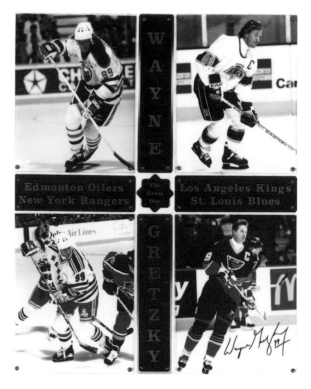

tive and intelligent puck handler with an acute awareness of where his teammates were, where the opponents were, and where everybody was going. Gretzky accumulated a remarkable 1,963 assists in his career—more assists than any other player in league history has points.

Gretzky played 20 seasons in the NHL, joining the Los Angeles Kings, the St. Louis Blues, and the New York Rangers after a nine-year stint with the Oilers.

In the end, he is known simply as the "Great One," and young hockey players everywhere scramble to wear uniform No. 99 like their idol.

Eddie Arcaro & Angel Cordero

When horse racing legend Eddie Arcaro retired after 31 years of competitive riding in 1961, Angel Cordero's racing career still was in its infancy in his native Puerto Rico. But the two men share a legacy that is the envy of most jockeys: their penchant for riding major race winners.

Arcaro had a record 17 winning mounts in Triple Crown races, including six Belmont Stakes winners, six Preakness winners, and five Kentucky Derby winners. He is the only jockey in history to ride two horses to the Triple Crown, sweeping the major races aboard Whirlaway in 1941 and Citation in 1948.

Cordero had six Triple Crown race winners, including three in the Preakness, two in the Belmont, and one in the Kentucky Derby. He added four first-place finishes in the prestigious Breeders' Cup.

Both jockeys are members of the National Museum of Racing's Hall of Fame.

No less an authority than the great Willie Shoemaker called Arcaro "the best rider I ever saw." Arcaro was just 22 when he won his

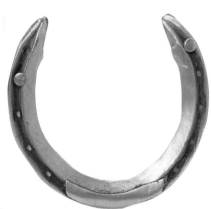

▲ This horseshoe was worn by Kelso, one of the greatest thoroughbred champions of all time.

Immortal Encounter

I spent many hours visiting Eddie Arcaro over the years at his Jockey Club apartment in Miami Beach, Florida. He was a fun-loving person who always seemed to be surrounded by beautiful women. Eddie and I often discussed his illustrious racing career. When I asked him to name the greatest horse he ever rode, Eddie said, without hesitation: "Citation."

My final encounter with Arcaro came six months before the legendary jockey passed away in 1997. It was at this meeting that Eddie presented me with the boots he wore when he rode Kelso in his last race.

We stood by his desk as he autographed the boots to the Sports Immortals Museum. Then he stood up and motioned for me to look out the window. He pointed to a building that was within walking distance of the Jockey Club. "See that house, Joel?" he whispered.

"Many times my good friends and I would take females there to party. If those walls could talk, what great tales could be told."

I laughed, then he continued. "You know, Joel, they wrote a book about me. But if I ever told the real stories about my life, between the pretty women and the offers to fix races, it would have been a best-seller."

I thanked my host for the boots and for the inside information, two items I would cherish for a long time. As Eddie walked me to the car, neither one of us knew it would be the last time we would see each other. Eddie waved good-bye and suggested that we call Joe DiMaggio to schedule a tee time to play golf in Boca Raton.

Sadly, that round of golf never happened. Eddie became ill and passed away a short time later.

—JOEL PLATT

▲ Arcaro (center) was among the five all-time great jockeys who signed this lithograph for Sports Immortals. Cordero's signature is on the left.

first Kentucky Derby aboard Lawring in 1938, and it was nearly two decades later that he won the last of his Triple Crown races, guiding Fabius (a son of Citation) in the 1956 Preakness. No other jockey has won the Preakness as many as six times.

In all, Arcaro won 4,779 races before retiring because of bursitis in his right arm. He won 554 stakes races, a record that stood until 1972, when Willie Shoemaker surpassed it.

That was just about the time that Cordero began forging his reputation in the major races. He won his first Kentucky Derby aboard Canonade in 1974, and two years later, won both the Preakness and the Belmont with Bold Forbes. His last win in a Triple Crown race came in 1985, when he rode Spend a Buck to victory in the Kentucky Derby.

▼ Eddie Arcaro, one of racing's greatest jockeys, presented these signed boots to Sports Immortals. Arcaro wore them in his last race aboard the great champion Kelso.

Cordero was the recipient of two Eclipse Awards as the jockey of the year (1982 and 1983), and retired in 1992 with 7,057 winning mounts, the fourth-best all-time mark.

CITATION

▲ Arcaro signed this photo of Citation. The great jockey steered Citation to the 1948 Triple Crown. The jockey called Citation "the greatest horse I ever rode."

▲ Angel Cordero signed this saddle, which he used while riding Canonade to victory in the 1974 Kentucky Derby.

Willie Shoemaker

They came to the top of the homestretch, and Willie Shoemaker was in the lead—right where he had finished an unbelievable 8,833 times in the 41 years since he began riding in 1949.

But Patchy Groundfog was the favorite only because the more than 64,000 fans in attendance had made him the sentimental choice, and in the end, Shoemaker couldn't keep him in front. The horse finished fourth, and his world-famous jockey called it a career.

It was billed as the "Legend's Last Ride," and it concluded a nine-month international farewell tour that took Shoemaker to four dozen tracks. From Spain to England to Germany to Sweden to the United States, Shoemaker made stops at tracks ranging from the grand to the dingy and everything in between.

Shoemaker was a transcontinental star, and the farewell tour was the brainchild of a New Zealand promoter who wanted to see the jockey go out with a bang. Shoemaker went along for the fun of it.

▲ The silks and hat were worn by Shoemaker while he rode Ferdinand to victory in the 1986 Kentucky Derby. The signed program is from his last ride in 1990.

"I didn't have to go on tour," he said. "I just wanted to."

And so he rode in London, Madrid, Zurich, Dusseldorf, and more . . . and on back to California, where it all started. He had his first winner at Golden Gate Fields, south of San Francisco, in 1949 (his last came at Florida's Gulfstream Park on January 20, 1990).

Shoemaker won 10 national money titles in his career, and rode horses that earned an astounding $123 million in purses. He won 11 Triple Crown races, including his fourth Kentucky Derby, aboard 17-1 longshot Ferdinand, at age 54 in 1986.

Shoemaker, who was paralyzed from the neck down in a single-car accident in 1991, rode more than 300 of his 1,009 career stakes winners at Santa Anita, the site of his last ride on February 3, 1990.

▲ Silks, cap, and boots that Shoemaker wore aboard Round Table.

He dismounted from Patchy Groundfog that day, his final competitive ride after more than four decades.

The very next morning, Shoemaker was up before dawn to head to the track—and begin his new career as a horse trainer. He was a special jockey who knew how to win.

Don Budge

▲ Photo of the great tennis champion, autographed "To Joel Platt, with my very best wishes, Don Budge."

Don Budge was born in Oakland, California, and developed his tennis game on the city's public courts. Gottfried von Cramm was a baron of German descent. But their disparate backgrounds took each of them to the top of the tennis profession: both had turns as the No. 1 player in the world in the late 1930s. And when they met at Wimbledon during a Davis Cup semifinal in 1937, they engaged in one of the greatest singles matches in the history of the event.

Just two weeks earlier, Budge had swept von Cramm in straight sets to win the singles final at Wimbledon. At the same site for the Davis Cup, Budge would win again—but it would not be so easy.

With the United States and Germany knotted at 2–2, Budge fell behind von Cramm in the decisive match, dropping the first two sets 6–8, 5–7. He came roaring back to win the next two, 6–4, 6–2, only to lose four of the first five games in the final set. After rallying again to take the lead, Budge was foiled on five

Immortal Encounter

I met Don Budge at his summer camp near Baltimore in 1975. When he finished teaching the children their morning lessons, I stopped him on his way off the court and introduced myself. After a few moments, he invited me to lunch. While we ate I told him about the explosion and my dream to develop a museum honoring outstanding athletic achievement. "Joel," he said, "it is evident you are focused on achieving your goal. Your museum will be a great motivation for youngsters. It would be my pleasure to help in any way possible."

I asked Don if I could obtain a racquet and clothing he used in one of his victories. He said, "I will forward the items to you as soon as I get back home."

When I asked him about his greatest moment of achievement in sports, he replied, "My greatest moment

came when I defeated the German Baron Gottfried von Cramm to help the United States defeat Germany in the 1937 Davis Cup semifinal. At the time, Hitler was preaching German supremacy, and the world was watching the outcome of my match with von Cramm and Joe Louis' fight for the heavyweight championship against Max Schmeling. I guess Joe and I showed the Fuhrer who was supreme."

I thanked Don for lunch and the interesting interview. Two weeks later, true to his word, Don forwarded the racquet and clothes he wore when winning the Wimbledon Doubles Championship.

—JOEL PLATT

Tennis

match points before winning the last set 8–6 to give the American team the victory.

▲ Tennis ball autographed to Joel Platt by Don Budge.

The United States went on to beat host Britain in the final to win its first Davis Cup title in 11 years. And Budge went on to become one of tennis' greatest legends.

In September 1937 Budge won the first of back-to-back U.S. Open titles, beating von Cramm again in a five-set final. He was named the *Associated Press* male athlete of the year and was the first tennis player to receive the Sullivan Award as the nation's top amateur athlete. Then, while still competing as an amateur in 1938, he became the first man ever to win the Grand Slam. In capturing the Australian, French, Wimbledon, and United States titles, Budge won all but five sets. He did not drop a single set at Wimbledon.

▲ Budge used this personalized racquet in the latter part of his career.

Amateur tennis still reigned in the years before World War II, but after having won all he could as an amateur, Budge began touring as a pro in 1939, and won a pair of U.S. pro titles. Three years later, he joined the air force and suffered a shoulder injury during training. Although he was no longer the dominating player he had been, players today are still chasing some of his records.

▼ In 1938, after Budge won the Grand Slam, amateur tennis officials had one of his shoes bronzed in tribute.

Don Budge Tennis Campus

Associate Director
BONNIE CROCKETT
275 Lincoln Ave.
Brentwood, New York 11717
516-231-7550

Owners · Directors
MR. & MRS. BUDGE
McDonogh, Maryland 21208
301-363-0600

August 17, 1975

To Joel Platt,

After much consideration, the toughest match I've ever played, under the most tense conditions, was the Davis Cup match against Baron Gottfried von Cramm in 1937 when the United States played Germany. Of all the tennis players I have ever seen I would have to say that the finest of all time have been Ellsworth Vines, Jack Kramer, Fred Perry, Bill Tilden, Gottfried von Cramm, Pancho Gonzalez, Lew Hoad and Rod Laver.

Sincerely,
Don Budge

▲ Budge sent this letter to Sports Immortals in 1975, calling his 1937 Davis Cup match with von Cramm his "toughest match."

Chris Evert

Teen tennis star Chris Evert was just 18 when she turned pro in 1972. By 1976 she was the first millionaire in women's tennis history, cashing in the first of what would become $9 million in career earnings.

That was on the court, anyway. Off it, Evert easily surpassed her first million in endorsements. Because from the time that she first arrived on the national scene as a 16-year-old amateur who reached the semifinals of the 1971 U.S. Open in Forest Hills with a quaint, two-handed backhand, she was America's Sweetheart, tennis' girl-next-door.

That made her an instant crowd favorite and a marketing manager's delight. Her performance on the court did not disappoint.

In 1974 Evert's Wimbledon title began a remarkable string in which she won at least one Grand Slam singles title for a record 13 consecutive years. She captured 157 singles titles in all and won 9 of every 10 career matches, including a string of 54 in a row in 1974. She was nearly unbeatable on clay, the surface on which she learned the game. She won the French Open seven times on clay, and once forged a 125-match winning streak on the surface.

Her style was sometimes called monotonous, a relentless barrage of baseline groundstrokes that wore down her foe. But you don't get style points in tennis, and her victories were a testament to the success of her style.

▲ Evert used this racquet while winning the 1976 Wimbledon singles championship.

▲ A painting by Yuri Liaboh of Martina Navratilova adorns the strings of this wooden racquet that Navratilova autographed.

▲ Martina Navratilova and Chris Evert created one of the best rivalries in tennis history, and two of the most amazing records of achievement.

Bjorn Borg

From 1976 to 1979, Bjorn Borg had owned Wimbledon, winning the world's most prestigious tennis tournament each time and equaling its modern record for consecutive victories. Now, in 1980, he faced his most formidable challenge yet in fiery 21-year-old American John McEnroe.

The two future Hall of Famers slugged it out in a grueling, five-set match that became as much a test of endurance as of skill. With Borg holding a two-sets-to-one advantage, they battled for 34 points in a historic, fourth-set tiebreaker in which Borg had five match points and McEnroe seven set points before McEnroe finally prevailed 18–16.

In the decisive fifth set, Borg called upon his trademark strength and determination to outlast McEnroe 8–6 and capture his fifth straight Wimbledon title in one of the most memorable finals ever.

By then Borg was a grizzled veteran at 24 years old. He had been just 16 when he made his Davis Cup debut for his native Sweden in 1972. He quickly rose to the top of the men's tennis world over the next decade, then just as quickly left the scene.

Borg was only 20—then the youngest champion in modern history—when he won Wimbledon for the first time in 1980. He went the entire tournament without losing a set, beating Ilie Nastase in the final.

By 1974 Borg was ranked among the top 10 in the world—and would stay there for eight years. He was No. 1 in 1979 and 1980. He would win 62 singles titles, including 11 majors, in his career. Along with his five Wimbledons, Borg won a record six French Open championships.

▲ Borg was the king of Wimbledon, tying a record by winning five consecutive times from 1976 to 1980. The final championship in that streak featured one of the most dramatic tennis matches ever, as Borg outlasted John McEnroe. Borg autographed this photo of him in action.

▲ Before switching to graphite later in his career, Borg used this wooden racquet. Also displayed is his trademark Fila warm-up jacket.

Andre Agassi vs. Pete Sampras

▲ Sports artist Yuri Liaboh created this unique look at the many faces of champion tennis player Andre Agassi.

It was not until after midnight in New York, when his 2001 U.S. Open quarterfinal victory over Andre Agassi was secured at last, that Pete Sampras could finally raise his arms in triumph.

The wonder was that Sampras could raise them at all after a grueling three-and-a-half-hour match fraught with suspense. "It always comes down to a couple of points with Andre," Sampras said afterward.

That was an understatement. Because on this night, Sampras had prevailed 6–7, 7–6, 7–6, 7–6 in one of the most taut and exciting matches in the history of U.S. Open tennis.

It was a classic match in a classic rivalry between two players who first began squaring off in junior tennis. Sampras had a slight edge in their professional matches, having won 17 times in 31 previous tries, though Agassi had won their three most recent meetings.

Sampras had four Open championships among his career-record 13 Grand Slam titles. But after losing to Russia's Marat Safin in the 2000 final at Flushing Meadows, he had suffered through a dismal 2001 season, and the Open was his last chance at extending a streak of nine consecutive years with at least one Grand Slam title. He was seeded just 10th, but beat former U.S. Open champion Patrick Rafter to advance against Agassi, another ex-champ.

▲ Agassi used this oversized Donnay racquet while winning the 1992 Wimbledon singles championship.

Agassi entered the match with seven major titles to his credit, including a pair of U.S. Opens; he had earned the second of his back-to-back Australian Open titles earlier in the year.

The two heavyweights battled to a 6–6 tie in each set, with neither player able to break the other's serve. After losing the first tiebreaker, Sampras won the final three, the last one 7–5.

Sampras would go on to defeat Safin in the semifinal before losing to Lleyton Hewitt in straight sets in the final. But the lingering memories of the 2001 U.S. Open will be of the titanic quarterfinal match with his longtime rival.

"It came down to the wire," Agassi said. "How much closer can you get?"

▲ This signed, used racquet was contributed to Sports Immortals by Pete Sampras.

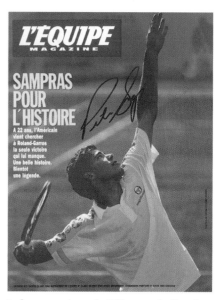

▲ Sampras autographed this copy of a French tennis magazine. His awesome record of Grand Slam victories has made him an international tennis favorite.

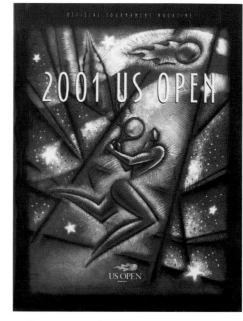

▲ Here is the colorful program from the historic 2001 U.S. Open, at which Sampras and Agassi dueled so memorably.

Richard Petty

Eight laps into the inaugural Daytona 500 in 1959, Richard Petty's car blew an engine. He was out of the race. Daytona International Speedway had just opened that year, but the 500 quickly became the crown jewel of NASCAR racing. Just as quickly, Petty recognized the importance of the race that is run annually in front of more fans than any other event in motor sports.

Though Petty's father, Lee, would go on to win that first 500, and though Richard would earn NASCAR rookie-of-the-year honors in 1959, the younger Petty knew you weren't really somebody in NASCAR until you won the "World's Greatest Race."

"Once you win Daytona, they start paying attention," he said. So he went about making the 500 his legacy.

Richard Petty won his first Daytona 500 in 1964. For the next 17 years he dominated the race, finishing with a record seven Daytona victories.

Petty's final victory at Daytona came in 1981, when he went into his last pit stop in fourth place. With only 25 laps left, Petty and his crew decided to forego changing tires. He raced to the front while the former leaders were changing their tires, and held off his pursuers to win in dramatic fashion.

But while Petty is best known for his performances at Daytona, they call him the "King" for much more than that. He won 200 NASCAR races in his career, nearly double

▼ NASCAR drivers go through several sets of tires in each race. This autographed tire was used on Petty's car during his final race in 1992.

that of the second-best mark (David Pearson's 105). He won a record seven Winston Cup championships (a mark eventually equaled by Dale Earnhardt). In 1967 Petty won 27 races, another record. And all the while, he remained accommodating and gracious to his legions of fans.

In 1984 President Ronald Reagan was on hand to witness Petty's final victory, a triumph in the Firecracker 400 at Daytona. Eight years later, President George H.W. Bush watched in Atlanta as Petty ended his driving career. Alas, Petty was forced from his final race after 95 laps when his car caught fire in a multicar wreck. But the racing legend was able to laugh it off.

"This wasn't the blaze of glory I wanted to go out in," he said.

▲ Petty wore this fireproof racing suit and goggles in 1991. The autographed suit shows the famous No. 43 logo of his car on the legs, along with the numerous sponsors who helped him ride to the top of the world of stock car racing.

▲ Petty's racing helmet shows the microphone system used to communicate with his pit crew. The helmet plugged into the in-car radio.

Dale Earnhardt

They called him the "Intimidator," and the nickname was well deserved by the man whose hard-driving racing style and gruff exterior made him at times both a hero and a villain on the NASCAR circuit.

But Dale Earnhardt could show his softer side, too, like when he entered Victory Lane in May 2000 to deliver a trademark bear hug to his son after Dale Earnhardt Jr. won The Winston in Concord, North Carolina.

And it was on the last lap of his last race, the Daytona 500 in February 2001, that the elder Earnhardt played the role of defender, not aggressor, running interference in third place for the two leaders, his son and Michael Waltrip, each of whom were driving cars the Intimidator owned.

However, on the last turn of the last lap, Earnhardt's well-known No. 3 car veered left down the track while being closely pursued, then abruptly turned right up the track and slammed into the wall head first. The tragic news came a short time later: Dale Earnhardt was dead at 49.

The death of one of the biggest legends in NASCAR history shook the sports world.

Earnhardt had been a fixture on the NASCAR circuit since 1979, when he was named the rookie of the year. The next season, he won the first of a record-tying seven Winston Cup championships. No other driver has won the rookie of the year and the Winston Cup series back-to-back.

▼ This helmet, signed by Earnhardt, Jeff Gordon, Dale Earnhardt Jr., and others commemorates NASCAR's 50th anniversary season in 1998.

Auto Racing

◀ A signed tire used in one of Earnhardt's races, an autographed, die-cast model of his famous black No. 3 car, and the cover of *The Sporting News* combine to form this Sports Immortals tribute to NASCAR's "Intimidator."

Earnhardt would go on to win more prize money than any other driver in NASCAR history. He finished among the all-time top 10 in starts, victories (he had 76), laps led, and top-five finishes.

But for all his success, Earnhardt's albatross was the Daytona 500. Though he won 29 races in different divisions or at different lengths at the Daytona International Speedway, it took him 20 starts in the "World's Greatest Race" before he won it in 1998. Three years later, going for another victory in the 500, he lost his life on the same track and millions of sports fans lost a hero.

▲ NASCAR teams sport matching shirts emblazoned with the names of sponsors. Earnhardt signed this shirt, which was later presented to Sports Immortals.

Pelé

On November 19, 1969, the Apollo 12 spacecraft landed on the moon, and man walked on the lunar surface for only the second time in history.

The same day, Brazilian soccer star Pelé scored his 1,000th career goal in a game at Rio de Janeiro's National Stadium.

In many parts of the world, the latter event was considered more significant.

Edson Arantes do Nascimento, better known to the world simply as Pelé, had been an international star—indeed, the world's biggest international star—ever since he burst onto the scene as a 17-year-old for the Brazilian national team at the 1958 World Cup in Sweden.

▲ Pelé autographed this game ball with his hand painted portrait.

Fans in Brazil, of course, already knew about the youngster who had left school at age 10 to pursue his dream of playing soccer. By the time he was 16, he was playing for the Santos Football Club, which he would lead to championships in each of his first six years and in 9 of 18 seasons overall.

Pelé didn't play in Brazil's opening 3–0 victory over Austria in the 1958 Cup, nor in a 0–0 tie with England. But he was on the field for a victory over the Soviet Union, then made the rest of the tournament his personal showcase.

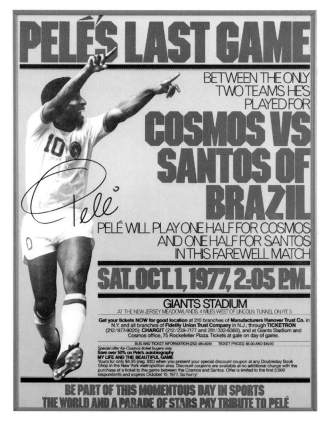

▲ Pelé played one half each for the Cosmos and his old Brazilian club, Santos, in his farewell match in 1977. Pelé autographed the poster after the game.

In the quarterfinals, his first career goal in the World Cup stood up for a 1–0 victory over Wales. Then he paced a 5–2 victory over France in the semifinals with a three-goal performance. He capped a remarkable debut with two goals in the final, another 5–2 victory over the host nation that lifted Brazil to its first World Cup title.

Pelé went on to help Brazil capture two more Cup titles, in 1962 and 1970. But after retiring from Santos in 1974, he took on an even bigger challenge—raising the profile of soccer in the United States. He signed with the North American Soccer League's New York Cosmos in 1975 and was the league's MVP in 1976. In 1977 the Cosmos won the NASL title.

A year later, Pelé retired for good. By some counts, he had as many as 1,280 career goals in 1,362 games. He has remained on the international scene as a goodwill ambassador.

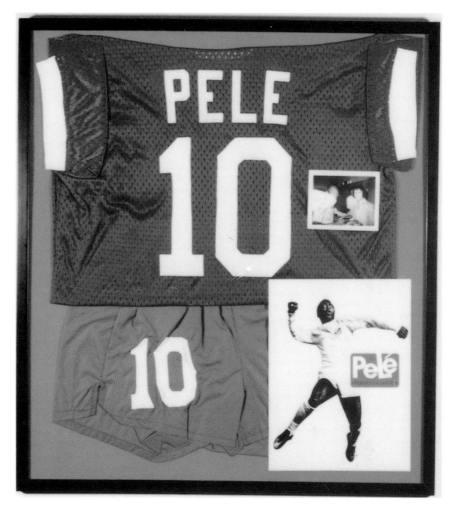

▲ With his outstanding goal-scoring abilities and his effervescent flair on and off the field, Pelé became the world's most famous athlete and his No. 10 uniform became synonymous with soccer greatness. Pictured above is Pelé's New York Cosmos uniform that was presented to Joel Platt.

Immortal Encounter

I met Pelé after practice in 1976, the year he was the MVP of the North American Soccer League. He invited me into the Cosmos locker room and we spoke about his three World Cup titles with Brazil in 1958, 1962, and 1970.

Pelé felt it would take several years, but that eventually soccer would become a popular sport in the United States.

When I showed Pelé the Sports Immortals Museum brochure and asked about obtaining a memento, he reached into his locker and presented me with his New York Cosmos game uniform.   —JOEL PLATT

Gallery

The Sports Immortals collection features more than one million mementos that will eventually be on display at a magnificent interactive museum attraction (see page 174 for more information). This Gallery section features a selection of rare and unique items from the vast collection.

Racing suit and gloves worn by Mario Andretti.

A pair of game jerseys from hockey legend Maurice "Rocket" Richard.

Lefty Grove, Philadelphia Athletics. 300 career wins, seven A.L. strikeout titles, nine ERA championships.

Sadaharu Oh, Tokyo Giants. World-record 868 home runs in his career. Game uniform signed by Oh and Hank Aaron.

Eric Dickerson ball, jersey, and helmet from 1984 game in which he reached a then-record single-season total of 2,007 rushing yards

Atlanta Braves jerseys of Hank Aaron, who hit a major league record 755 career home runs.

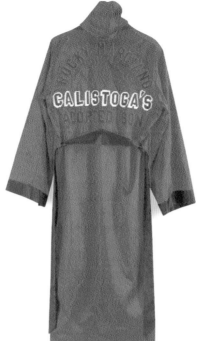

Philadelphia Eagles linebacker Chuck Bednarik wore this jersey when he played more than 58 minutes in the 1960 NFL Championship Game. The Eagles defeated the Green Bay Packers 17–13.

After training in Calistoga, California, Rocky Marciano got this robe from grateful local residents and wore it in his championship fight against Don Cockell on May 16, 1955.

Game jersey of Sammy Baugh, Washington Redskins. Six-time passing champion. Led NFL in passing, punting, and interceptions in 1943.

Game uniforms from 1973 NBA-champion New York Knicks: Bill Bradley, Willis Reed, Earl Monroe, Jerry Lucas, Walt Frazier, and Dave Debusschere.

Willie Mays game jerseys from the New York Giants, the San Francisco Giants (with hat and card), and the New York Mets.

Signed by more than 125 Hall of Fame players, this is the most valuable signed bat in existence. Signatures include those of Roberto Clemente, Jackie Robinson, Mel Ott, Ty Cobb, and more.

Autographed first baseman's mitt used by New York Giants great Bill Terry.

One of only three single-signature baseballs from Adrian "Cap" Anson, one of the top players of the 1800s.

Baseball signed by the original inductees of the Baseball Hall of Fame in 1939: Ruth, Cobb, Wagner, Collins, Speaker, Young, Johnson, Mack, Sisler, Lajoie, and Alexander.

Joe Jackson autographed baseball from 1917 World Series.

Baseball signed by 1930 Homestead Grays, including Josh Gibson and Oscar Charleston.

The Ball Room

Last ball used in 1917 double no-hitter pitched by the Reds' Fred Toney and the Cubs' Hippo Vaughn. Reds won in 10.

Joel Platt in his unique "ball room" in 1974. The room featured more than 6,000 autographed balls dating to 1865.

Baseball signed by Don Larsen from his 1956 World Series perfect game.

Jack Johnson's boxing glove autographed by many of boxing's greatest champions.

Letter from Babe Ruth to Connie Mack on Mack's 80th birthday in 1942.

Christmas card signed by 1800s baseball stars George Wright and Albert G. Spalding.

Oversized boxing glove signed by hundreds of the biggest names of boxing, including Dempsey, Ali, Louis, Willard, Frazier, Foreman, Root, Sharkey, Zale, Ross, Tunney, Jeffries, and more.

Confession letter signed by boxing legend Jack Johnson stating that he threw the fight against Jess Willard.

Letter written from Honus Wagner to young lady who requested one of Wagner's bats.

Bronko Nagurski's 1934 contract with the Chicago Bears. He was paid $225 per regular-season game (and nothing for exhibition games).

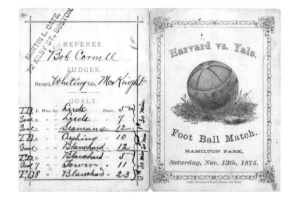

Late 1800s baseball scorecards.

Souvenir program from Davis Cup competition in 1913.

1875 program from Baltimore Baseball Club.

Program from the first Harvard vs. Yale football game in 1875.

Program from the 1919 championship fight between Jess Willard and Jack Dempsey.

Program from a July 4, 1907, championship fight between Tommy Burns and Billy Squires.

Program from 1908 championship fight between Joe Gans and Battling Nelson.

Program from 1923 championship fight between Jack Dempsey and Luis Firpo.

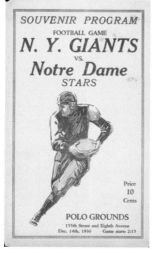

1930 exhibition football game between the New York Giants and Notre Dame.

Program from 1936 exhibition in Cuba between the New York Giants and the St. Louis Cardinals.

Program from championship fight between Jack Johnson and Tommy Burns held in Sydney, Australia.

Program from an exhibition between the New York Yankees and the Johnstown (PA) Baseball Club, 1927.

Program from championship fight between Robert Fitzsimmons and Jim Corbett.

Program from championship fight between James Jeffries and Robert Fitzsimmons in 1902.

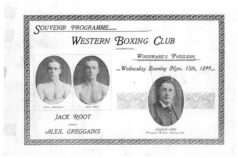

1899 program from bout between Jack Root and Alex Greggains.

1974 All-Star Game program autographed by players from both leagues.

Program from the 1933 World Series between the Washington Senators and the New York Giants.

Program from 1973 fight between Joe Frazier and George Foreman.

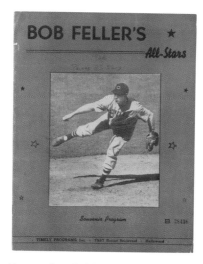

Program from Bob Feller's traveling All-Star team in 1946.

Hand-painted mug presented to early football pioneer Walter Camp in 1880.

Lucky horseshoe made by boxing champion Bob Fitzsimmons, along with autographed photo.

These are the first ice skates patented in the U.S., from 1864.

Championship belt presented to Owen Moran in 1908.

Vase autographed by Babe Ruth during 1935 all-star team tour of Japan.

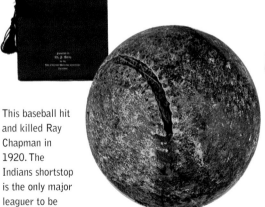

This baseball hit and killed Ray Chapman in 1920. The Indians shortstop is the only major leaguer to be killed on the field. At top is a program from his memorial.

This is the actual home plate from the Polo Grounds that New York Giants outfielder Bobby Thomson stepped on after hitting his dramatic "Shot Heard 'Round the World" home run to win the 1951 National League pennant

Gallery: Unique Items

Bare-knuckles champion Tom Sayers is depicted in this rare lithograph; the silver plate was presented to Sayers by the British Prime Minister in 1860.

This watch was presented to President William Howard Taft at the opening of Cincinnati's Redlands Park in 1912.

A collection of period drawings of bare-knuckle boxing champions from the 1800s.

A baseball from a game played in 1865 by the Monitor Baseball Club.

Horseshoe worn by Triple Crown winner Secretariat.

Horseshoe worn by another great champion, Man O' War.

Trophy presented to heavyweight boxing champion James J. Jeffries in 1938.

A baseball-themed clock from the late 1800s.

Peter Jackson, and 1890s boxing champion, signed this photo, along with a program and card from one of his fights.

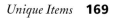

Honus Wagner "T206" baseball card, the most valuable in the world.

Early 1900s sterling silver medallions that served as annual passes to New York Giants games. The above passes were issued to Governor John Tener, later president of the N.L.

PLANK, PHILA. AMER.

Rare "T206" card of Philadelphia Hall of Fame pitcher Ed Plank.

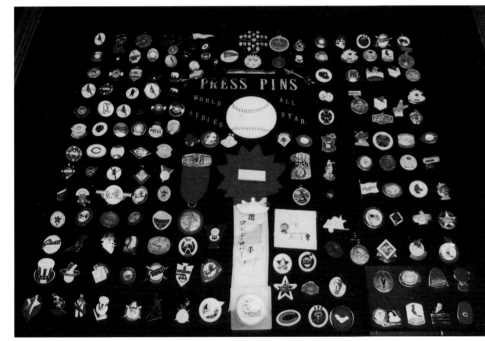

World Series and All-Star game press pin collection dating back to 1911.

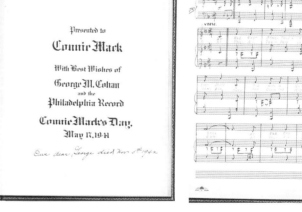

Original sheet music for a song written by George M. Cohan to celebrate Connie Mack Day, May 17, 1941.

1920 World Series Championship pin presented to Tris Speaker, Hall of Fame outfielder for the Cleveland Indians.

Gallery: Cards, Tickets, and Pins

A collection of tickets and ticket stubs from the most famous championship boxing events of the century.

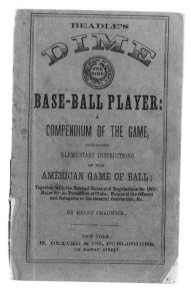

Handbook about the "American Game of Ball," published in 1860 by early baseball writer Henry Chadwick, the "Grandfather of Baseball."

1909-11 Colgan's Chips, Stars of the Diamond.

Early 1900s sheet music for song "Hurray for Our Baseball Team."

Complete set of the first sports cards issued by the Allen & Ginter Co. in 1887.

Cy Young, Christy Mathewson, and Ty Cobb are pictured on these Sweet Caporal Premium pins from 1910.

Honus Wagner Day photo button.

Baseball coin from 1858.

Press ticket from the 1927 World Series between the New York Yankees and the Pittsburgh Pirates.

"Two Worlds" pictures Dan Marino at the University of Pittsburgh and with the Miami Dolphins. It was painted by Robert Stephen Simon.

"The Greatest," featuring Michael Jordan and Muhammad Ali and painted by Yuri Liaboh.

"Home Run Kings" features long-ball champs Mark McGwire, Sammy Sosa, Barry Bonds, and Babe Ruth. The painting is an original by Yuri Liaboh.

Jack Dempsey

Walter Hagen

Amelia Earhart

Paavo Nurmi

Ty Cobb

Suzanne Langlen

These one-of-a-kind dolls were created for a display on heroes from the world of sports and other fields put on at the 1933 Chicago World's Fair.

Gene Sarazen

Jim Thorpe

Gene Tunney

Helen Wills Moody

Duke Kahanamakou

Charles Lindbergh

This painting of Joe DiMaggio and Honus Wagner by artist Yuri Liaboh expresses the important sentiment of helping young people achieve their dreams.

Yankees slugger Mickey Mantle signed this original painting of Mantle and Dodgers star catcher Roy Campanella in the 1956 World Series by Robert Stephen Simon.

The Sports Immortals Museum

Sports Immortals is solely devoted to the super athletes whose impacts on sports never fade from our view. It is a project that conjures up the roar of the crowd, the pinnacle of performance, the unmatched rapport between athlete and fan, and, most importantly, preserves the memories and achievements of the world's greatest athletes.

MAJOR COMPONENTS

Interactive Museum

The focal point of the Sports Immortals Experience will be the Sports Immortals Museum, an inspirational attraction that will celebrate the accomplishments of sports history's timeless heroes. Presented in chronological order, each era of sports will come to life. Through the use of the latest multimedia technology, visitors will hear the sounds and see the sights of the times. For example, the 1920s will feature Vaudeville music and contain animated wax figures and mementos from Babe Ruth, Bill Tilden, Bobby Jones, Jack Dempsey, Knute Rockne, etc. With the emotion and the drama of the moment, every visitor will be able to relive his/her favorite period in sports history.

Restaurant of Champions

The Sports Immortals Gallery and Grill Restaurant will incorporate the best in sports, interactive entertainment, creative retail, celebrity appearances, and best of all, excellent food. There will also be a Sky Box Café for those in a hurry and looking for ballgame fare.

Sports Retail

This retail component will provide the visitor with an opportunity to purchase rare collectibles, licensed merchandise from all major sports, and specially created Sports Immortals–branded products, such as apparel, prints, statues, toys, games, books, and more.

Interactive Arcade

Visitors will compete in interactive sports competitions with one another and against "Virtual Sports Immortals." By utilizing the latest technology, participants will be able to race against Lance Armstrong, stand toe to toe with Muhammad Ali, hit a Nolan Ryan fastball, strike out Babe Ruth, or kick the winning field goal in the Super Bowl. In addition, Sports Immortals will feature a "You Make the Call" exhibit where visitors can call the play by play from some great moments in sports.

Immortals Cinema

Sports Immortals will feature a 360-degree theater that will show the 20 greatest moments in sports history. There will also be a multimedia theater where visitors can watch various Hollywood classics that pay tribute to the Sports Immortals, such as *Jim Thorpe: All American*, *The Knute Rockne Story*, and many more.

AN INTERVIEW WITH JOEL PLATT

What is your ultimate mission and goal for the Sports Immortals project?

My mission is to develop an interactive Smithsonian-type attraction that would perpetuate the memories and achievements of the greatest athletes in sports history. The ultimate goals for Sports Immortals are as follows:

- to make enshrinement as a Sports Immortal one of the greatest honors that can be achieved in sports
- to establish a foundation that would contribute to sports medicine research and related organizations
- to inspire and motivate every visitor to strive for maximum effort in his or her life endeavors

How will the Sports Immortals Experience differ from existing Halls of Fame?

Sports Immortals will be different in three major ways:

1. Our attraction will be located in a major city/tourist market whereas existing Halls of Fame locations were based on history, rather than on maximizing the number of potential visitors.
2. We will enshrine the greatest athletes of all major sports.
3. We will use state-of-the-art technology and interactive displays.

How can the public participate in the development of Sports Immortal projects?

- tax deductible donations to the Platt Sports Foundation (monetary contributions or donations of rare sports mementos)
- corporate sponsorships and naming rights
- as investors

Is any of your memorabilia available to be seen by the public, or will they have to wait until the Sports Immortals Experience is developed?

We have established our Sports Immortals Showcase Museum in Boca Raton, Florida, to serve as a preview to our Sports Immortals Experience. The facility features rotating displays of over 20,000 mementos. It also offers a selection of over 10,000 non-museum-related items to purchase in our state-of-the-art memorabilia mart. In addition our website, www.sportsimmortals.com, offers a selection of items to see and purchase.

How have you managed to stay focused all your life on achieving your dream?

I have always structured my life by a set of rules and values that I have compiled into the "Sports Immortals Rules for Success."

- **Never lose sight of your dreams.**
- **Set goals for yourself.**
- **Always give maximum effort.**
- **Never be afraid of failure.**
- **Learn from your mistakes.**
- **Keep physically fit.**
- **Avoid drugs.**
- **Be flexible and tolerant.**
- **Believe in yourself.**
- **Have faith and trust your instincts.**

For more information:

Sports Immortals, Inc./Platt Sports Foundation, Inc.
6830 N. Federal Highway
Boca Raton, FL 33487
(561) 997-2575
www.sportsimmortals.com

Ed Calesa & Blue
Testament to Perseverance

Sports Immortals is a story that demonstrates the importance of perseverance and a "can do" attitude. It truly shows that there are no barriers to our achievement except those that we impose upon ourselves. I believe this to be the case for humans, as well as animals—in particular, my horse, Blue.

She was not an expensive horse and I was not an experienced rider. Together we made a great team. After watching a video on how to teach a horse how to cut, Blue and I went into training at my new ranch in Weatherford, Texas. Our goal was simple: to win the annual Cutting Horse Futurity event.

Because I had never entered an event like this before, it would seem that ours was an unattainable goal. But I did not think so. I always stayed positive and believed in achieving my aim. However I knew that I needed an edge to be able to compete successfully.

The edge that I used was to build trust, confidence, and a relationship with this horse such that she would always know she could rely on me. I tried to build her confidence by never letting her experience failure. I let Blue grow and develop in the sport and gave her the opportunity to take risks. I never made the mistake of thinking I could teach her but, rather, encouraged her to experience her own ability and express that ability without the barriers that confine so many people or animals or entities on this earth.

All of my effort seemed to be working until the middle of the Futurity year, when I was informed that Blue was sick, and we needed a vet. After examining the horse, the vet told me that she had colic and would die, and that there was nothing he could do. I told him that this horse could not die. He suggested taking her to a surgical center seven hours away but indicated that in his professional opinion she would not live for seven hours, especially in a trailer traveling that distance. But he was wrong. I didn't accept his definition of the outcome. When we arrived at the surgical center, the surgeon on staff refused to operate on the horse because he told me she would not live through the operation. I asked him to operate anyway.

Blue survived the operation and made an incredible recovery. We spent a lot of time together over the next several months, not as horse and rider, but as friends. We did everything together except ride. I did not attempt to mount her until two weeks before the Futurity. The vet thought I was crazy to think of still entering her in the event, but I did it anyway.

We started off slowly. Then I increased her exercise level every day. I did not put her in front of cattle, because that was stressful, until three days before the event. When the time came and they called our name to perform, I whispered in her ear that we were about to do something that had never been done before. Therefore, let's go in and win.

▲ Ed Calesa rides Blue in the 1994 Cutting Horse Spectacular in Las Vegas.

Blue competed brilliantly. We made it to the semifinals and ultimately finished 21st. She was amazing. Blue not only conquered her illness, but she also became a champion. After this event, Blue never finished below the top 10 in any competition.

I learned several lessons from my time with Blue. First, it is motivating to see people perform to their maximum ability when they recognize that there are no restrictions or barriers to their own success. Second, it's incredible what people can do when they overcome obstacles and persevere to achieve their goals. By never giving up, individuals can experience the precious gift of life—living.

—*Ed Calesa*

Index

Author Acknowledgments

Ed Calesa

Marcia Platt	Robert & Madylene Platt	Dalia Platt
Tim Alexander	Robert Ardolino	James Armstrong
Bruce Bernstein	Richard Brooks	Charles R. Davies
Craig Dunoff	Harry D. Evans	Tommy Farmer
Buddy Feldshon	Frank Fiore	Francis Flanagan
Jim Gdula	Shari, Jordanna & Jake Glatter	Eric Gold
Phil "Chappy" Goldstein	Dr. Joseph Haller	Franco Harris
Dennis Heindl	Don & Todd Hewitt	Chad Horne
Barry Howard	Blair Jacobson	Dave Jordano
Jack Kemp	Emil Klosinski	Jeffrey J. Kraws
Rabbi Harold Kushner	Max & Sophie Leff	Yuri Liaboh
Mark Littman	Michael & Alice Lopota	Maurice Lucas
Ron Mahoney	Thomas McGillicuddy	John Murphy
Rocky Platt	Dave Reierson & Tim Utech	Ed Rowlands
Cong. E. G. "Bud" Shuster	Matt Silk	Robert Stephen Simon
Abe and Ron Steinberg	Bernie Stumpf	Grace Thorpe
Roger Trevino	Irwin B. Wedner	David Werth
Jaime & Mina Wielgus	Wendy & Michael Wilson	Tyler, Jennifer & Juliet Wilson
Ivo Zini	Robert & Marlene Zukerman	Ernie and Liz Banks

Shoreline Publishing Group LLC thanks the following for their invaluable assistance
in the preparation of this book: designer Eileen Wagner for her perseverance;
writer and editor Jim Gigliotti; Tish O'Connor and Dana Levy of Perpetua Press;
Mitch Rogatz, Tom Bast, and Blythe Hurley of Triumph Books.